Amber River

a guidebook to unique pubs of Vancouver Island and the Salish Sea

GLEN COWLEY

hancock

house

83

71

80-82

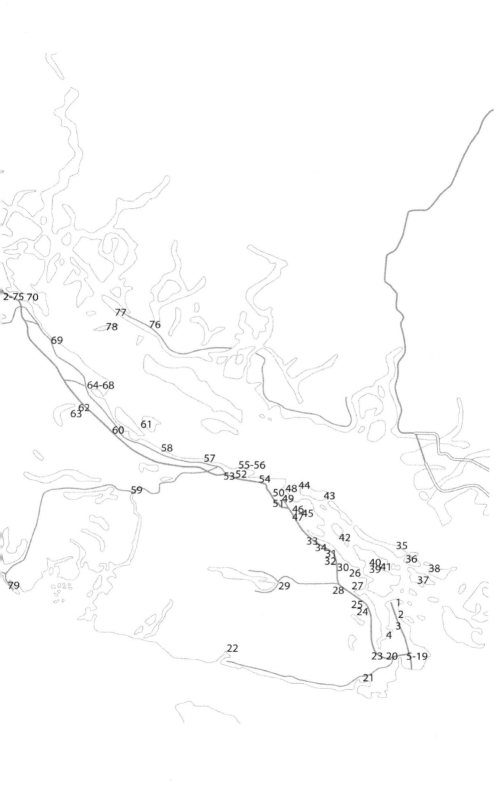

ISBN-13: 978-0-88839-075-2 [trade softcover]
Copyright © 2018 Glen Cowley

Library and Archives Canada Cataloguing in Publication

Cowley, Glen, 1949-, author
Amber river : a guidebook to the pubs of Vancouver Island and the
Salish Sea / Glen Cowley.

ISBN 978-0-88839-075-2 (softcover)

1. Bars (Drinking establishments)--British Columbia—Vancouver
Island--Guidebooks. 2. Bars (Drinking establishments)--Salish Sea (B.C.
and Wash.)--Guidebooks. 3. Guidebooks. I. Title.

TX950.59.C3C69 2018   647.95711'2   C2018-904112-9

Copyediting: D. Martens
Production & Design: M. Lamont

Front Cover Images: Courtesy of Moon Under Water Brewpub

*We acknowledge the financial support of the Government of Canada through the
Canada Book Fund for our publishing activities.*

Printed in the USA

Published simultaneously in Canada and the United States by

HANCOCK HOUSE PUBLISHERS LTD.
19313 Zero Avenue, Surrey, BC Canada V3S 9R9
(604) 538-1114 Fax (604) 538-2262

HANCOCK HOUSE PUBLISHERS
#104 4550 Birch Bay-Lynden Rd, WA, USA 98230-5005
(800) 938-1114 Fax (800) 983-2262

Website: **www.hancockhouse.com**
Email: **sales@hancockhouse.com**

Amber
River

a guidebook to unique pubs of Vancouver Island and the Salish Sea

GLEN COWLEY

Contents

1. VICTORIA/SOUTH VANCOUVER ISLAND:
North Saanich, Saanichton, Sidney...

2. MID-ISLAND SOUTH:
Cobble Hill, Chemainus, Maple Bay, Duncan, Ladysmith...

3. THE GULF ISLANDS:
Galiano, North Pender, Salt Spring, Gabriola, Mayne, Thetis...

4. NANAIMO:
Nanaimo & Protection Island

5. MID-NORTH ISLAND:

Parksville, Qualicum, Fanny, Hornby, Comox, Campbell River...

6. SUNSHINE COAST
Powell River, Lund, Savary Island...

7. WEST COAST
Ucluelet & Tofino

8. NORTH ISLAND
Telegraph Cove, Malcolm Island & Port Hardy

INTRODUCTION

Historically, the life blood of pubs has been beer, an amber river flowing since the age of the ancient Sumerians. Though pubs have expanded into the realm of fine foods, wine, ciders, liquor and entertainment, the beer essence of these communal gathering spots has persisted. On Vancouver Island and about the Salish Sea neighbourhood, pubs branded with their own uniqueness and wedded to the offerings of their locales have evolved to become destinations in and of themselves.

Amber River presents a collection of such pubs and their connection to their locales.

The idea for this guidebook arose from a longstanding practice my wife, Karen, and I have followed, when venturing out for a day or a more extended sojourn, of incorporating respite at a pub, coffee shop or restaurant featuring an element of individuality—a break from franchises and commonality. Seeking uniqueness has become a bit of a habit for us, and it struck me in chatting with others that this is a not unappreciated practice.

The result is a guidebook to 85 pubs or pub-style restaurants, accompanied by suggestions (under the "Earning Your Beer" section) on activities and experiences to be enjoyed in the immediate area.
Some pubs are marked by a singularly unique feature, such as a stunning view—not uncommon in a province as heavily blessed with scenery as British Columbia. However, many have numerous elements that merit special attention: setting, history, location, architecture, interior decor, themes, Island craft beers on tap, brew pubs, intriguing stories, landscaping, physical features, and atmosphere. A host of combinations make these attractive.

From basic pub fare to higher end dining, food has become a major part of pub operations these days, in some cases taking precedence over the serving of alcohol. Not being endowed with the requisite skills to assess cuisine, I leave such to the experts; however, I would say I have not been displeased with any meals and have been singularly impressed by some.

It should be noted that uniqueness is very much subject to context, and that makes comparisons virtually impossible. The opulence of Victoria's Bard and Banker contrasts sharply with the rustic appeal of the Whale's Rub Pub in Sointula on Malcolm Island, the enigmatic appeal of the haunted Black Goose Pub near Parksville, the floating Dinghy Dock Pub of Nanaimo, or the compelling view from the Lion Rampant at Maple Bay. They all have their own attractions marking them as special places to visit and experience and, for those blessed with having them nearby, to take visitors to.

The marriage of pubs to activities and experiences enhances both. Whether it's a cool craft beer at the Cobblestone Inn after a healthy climb up Cobble Hill; a refreshing break at the Rumrunner Pub in Sidney, gazing over the waters to the United States on the horizon after a cycling excursion on the Galloping Goose and Lochside Trail; or local-food dining at the Cowichan Bay Pub after exploring shops, galleries, and museums in Cowichan Bay, it all combines for a pleasing day. Expand your visit for a weekend or longer and the hinterland offerings expand proportionately, for a greater appreciation of time and place. Whale-watching tours from Telegraph Cove piggyback on grizzly bear viewing excursions, topped by a view-enriched visit to the Old Saltery Pub; mountain biking, hiking and savouring the sunset are enhanced by jazz strains at the Thatch Pub on Hornby Island; beach walks, bird watching and serenity can be capped by a community evening at Riggers on isolated, sand-framed Savary Island.

Given the many unique elements of these pubs, you can even make them a part of a themed road trip. Kayakers can cruise the Gulf Islands enjoying put-ins at the beachfront Surf Pub on Gabriola, Port Browning Pub on North Pender, or history-laden Springwater Lodge, to name but a few. Ghost hunters can run the gamut in Victoria, from 17 Mile House through 6 Mile House, 4 Mile House, Christie's, and the characterful Bent Mast in James Bay. Similar excursions are possible whatever your interests, for golfers, birders, naturalists, cyclists, boaters, architecture and history buffs, craft beer aficionados, music lovers, festival followers, mountain bikers, photographers, scuba divers, surfers and more. For motorcyclists and car clubbers who enjoy windy, scenic drives, there are routes to be enjoyed with an evening-ending pub visit to compare notes.

For easy planning, this guidebook provides lots of contact information, websites and links. Of course, things do change, so before heading out for that special trip, make use of those resources to get the most out of your adventures and visits. Taking the time to check tourist information sites and pick up or download maps and brochures can do much to enhance the experience. Perhaps you'll find that little surprise that can add so much to a trip.

It's equally important to remember that hiking and biking on the Island will often take you into near-wilderness, and you should heed cautions about respecting wildlife and other potential dangers, such as rogue waves. It's always a good practice to let someone know where you are going and to ensure you have basic necessities with you.

Researching this book has been pleasant, for both the activities I've experienced and the hours spent pub savouring, which brought enough pleasure to draw me back again and again. Every time we visit a place and pub, I am delighted to learn something new, an experience I'm sure others will share when they visit.

Cheers!
Glen Cowley

GUIDE TO THE GUIDE

The guidebook isn't designed to rate various pubs, but rather to recognize the unique elements that make certain pubs especially worthy of a visit. Some pubs we visited weren't that appealing, others did not want to be in the book, and, most significantly, the numbers kept growing to the point that a cut-off mark had to be established. So, there are more unique pubs out there still awaiting discovery!

Here's an explanation of how this guidebook is set up and how you might use it:

1. Identification and Contact Information
   Having made a special trip to visit a pub, nobody wants to be disappointed, either by not finding it, or by discovering its hours or services have changed. The contact information, initial photo and location information are provided so you can double-check on hours and services, especially if you're entertaining the idea of a road trip.

2. The Narrative
   This is the story of the pub, a description and commentary on what makes it unique, plus its relationship to the Island and to its local community. Do take note of those unique features, because patrons invariably discover new features not specifically mentioned in the book. Enjoy your own adventure of discovery.

3. Earning Your Beer
   This section suggests an activity or activities, often hikes, to incorporate into your pub visit to make for a more fulfilling day.

4. Stamp Box
   Here's something of special interest to collectors and those who have ambitions of visiting all the pubs in this guide. This box marks

a spot in each listing where you can get a souvenir endorsement, be that a stamp or a signature, to prove you've visited each pub.

5. The George Orwell Questionnaire

Back in the 1940s, George Orwell (famed author of 1984 and Animal Farm) wrote an essay defining his ideal pub. I've assembled 15 points from the essay into a questionnaire that will allow you to do your own assessments of various pubs to see which most closely approximate Orwell's ideal. Besides being fun, this exercise will help you observe and learn more about the pub.

Amber River is meant to be a fun book with a positive bent, one that encourages discovery of unique places on beautiful Vancouver Island and its environs. I hope those who read it enjoy it in that vein.

THE ORWELL TEST FROM "MOON UNDER WATER"

1. *Is it close to or does it provide transportation?*

2. *Is it free of rowdies and drunks?*

3. *Are there regular clientele there for conversation as much as for drinks?*

4. *Does it have "atmosphere"?*

5. *Does it have architectural appeal?*

6. *Does it have a wood fire?*

7. *Does it have plenty of elbow room?*

8. *Does it have a games room or dedicated area?*

9. *Does it have a section quiet enough to talk?*

10. *Do the servers know the regulars by name?*

11. *Do they serve snacks at the bar and have meals available?*

12. *Do they have draught stout?*

13. *Do they have handled beer glasses (ideally china)?*

14. *Do they have a garden or outside grounds?*

15. *Do they have a section for families with children?*

SECTION ONE Victoria & South Vancouver Island

ESTABLISHMENT 1

The Stonehouse Pub

2215 Canoe Cove Road, North Saanich

1-778-351-1133

Website –   stonehousepub.ca

Services –   wi-fi, wheelchair-accessible with wheel
chair-accessible washrooms

Location

Driving on the Patricia Bay Highway #17, prior to the ferry at Swartz Bay, follow signs to exit 33 to Canoe Cove. Just before reaching the cove and marina, you will see a sign directing you to the right. The Stonehouse is nestled, with all the charm of an English country house, amid gardens and tended groves.

What makes the Stonehouse Pub unique: architecture, setting, location and gardens

The Stonehouse Pub appears to grow from the bones of the Earth itself, like the inspiring cottage of a famed playwright, full of reflective atmosphere. Solid stone touched in Tudor style, with steeply pitched rooflines, heavily embraced by vine and bush, it much suits its name. This English-style manor house was constructed in the 1930s by businessman Hugh Rood and his family, recently of Great Britain. Constructed from locally quarried stone with hand-hewn beams, leaded glass and fir floors, the house, first named "The Landing," was grand from the start. It began its new life as a pub under the moniker "Stone House" in 1985.

A major part of the manor was its gardens, walkways and grounds, and these continue to be outstanding features of the pub, which has two outdoor patios hugging the rocky hillside.

The grounds retain an edge of the wild about them, such as could tempt the imagination and spawn creativity. Places of quiet solitude, where birdsong echoes, offer a nice place to sit outdoors, watch and listen. The small indoor pub section adjoining the restaurant carries an air of polished, comfortable modernity, with ample views of the outside. The beams, leaded glass and fir floors catch the eye and recall the home's origins.

Some 95% of the taps are set to craft beers, including products of the Vancouver Island, Lighthouse, Phillips and Driftwood breweries, all of Victoria. Patron services include shuttle bus and wheelchair accessibility. It's the type of place where a writer could draw inspiration, through quiet attentiveness to the surrounding sights and sounds, or where an eased mind could wander its own meandering path. Yet it remains equally inviting for groups who want to relax in appreciative company after a day spent hiking, biking or cruising the waters.

Earning your beer

The Stonehouse Pub is bike-friendly, with outside racks, and for good reason. The 29-kilometre Lochside Regional Trail begins or ends here, depending on your intentions. Hikers can work up a healthy appetite and thirst with a hike or bike in from Sidney. For directions, web-check Lochside Regional Trail. Doable in roughly 17 minutes on a bike, the trail stretches to an hour and a quarter by foot.

Visitors might also like to take in the marina at the foot of a series of steps just below the pub, camouflaged by a stand of trees. Eco-tours are conducted out of the marina, as is water taxi service to Portland Island and Sidney Spit, both part of the Gulf Islands National Park system. You can spend a day hiking Portland Island or Sidney Spit and finish off at the Stonehouse. Check out the site ecocruising.com.

Mainland visitors can even come in as foot passengers, as the pub and the marina are but a short walk from the ferry terminal in Swartz Bay.

ESTABLISHMENT 2

The Rumrunner

9881 Seaport Place, Sidney

1-250-656-5643

Webpage – rumrunnerpub.ca

Services – wi-fi, wheelchair-accessible with wheel chair-accessible washrooms.

Location

Take Sidney's Beacon Avenue towards the sea to the roundabout, swing off on Seaport Place, and look for the building with the beacon, next to the breakwater.

<u>What makes the Rumrunner unique:</u> location, setting, view and architecture

There was adventure on these shores back in the days of Prohibition in the United States—adventure recalled in the name of Sidney's Rumrunner Pub and in the stained-glass panel above the bar. Today, under its lighthouse beacon, you can enjoy a fine brew and meal while gazing upon the islands and mainland of our southern neighbours across the waters. What stories could be told about the days when the cat-and-mouse game of rumrunning was played!

Craft such as the Malahat and the Revuocnav (Vancouver spelled backwards) dodged hijackers, the U.S. federal authorities and the Mounties in their mission to slake the thirst of a despairingly dry populace to our south.

The many-windowed interior of the pub and its seasonal outdoor patios offer stunning views of Washington State's near shores, the San Juan Islands, towering Mount Baker and the Olympic Range. A brick seaside

promenade running above the breakwater is embellished with maritime artistry and tended lawns, while nearby the tinkle of rope slapping against masts betrays the presence of the sheltered Port Sidney Marina. Bar, bench and table and chair seating accommodate group gatherings, as well as singles and couples seeking private conversation. The maritime theme is carried throughout the pub and is augmented by a warming fireplace and a couple of sports-oriented TVs. Publican Bill Singer put thought and effort into creating atmosphere when he built the Rumrunner back in 1990, and it shows today in the pub/restaurant operation that opens this scenic viewpoint peninsula to adults and families.

Upon the walls, a photo of the immediate shoreline in a temper tantrum shares space with a special Raeside cartoon featuring Bill when he worked at the famous old Snug Pub. For those who recall the story of the cougar in the Empress Hotel parking lot, the panel evokes a knowing chuckle. The wood-accented interior evokes a sense of space and light everywhere, allowing the outside in. The view is focussed upon a sea dotted with sails, and not a car to be seen.

Located in the town of Sidney by the Sea, the Rumrunner and its patrons are served by a quality bus service, providing ease of mind when enjoying the refreshing offerings of bar and table. The taps afford plenty of local flavour, with craft beers from Victoria's craft breweries Lighthouse, Phillips, and Vancouver Island, as well as time-honoured Guinness. It is easy to picture the old rumrunner nursing a glass of amber, staring out across the waters, enjoying the warmth of the fireplace and recalling the heady days of smuggling adventure.

Earning your beer

Sidney, and the Rumrunner's location in its heart, offer a wealth of experiences on foot or by bus. Right near the Rumrunner, the annual sail-past draws visitors, as do markets and walkways like the two-kilometre seaside promenade and the 29-kilometre Lochside Trail, which connects with the Galloping Goose Trail. Known as a book-lover's town, Sidney houses nine bookstores carrying new and used books. Bike or hike or saunter, there is lots to see and do before or after enjoying the offerings of the Rumrunner. Boat tours of varying sorts, including eco-tours and whale-watching, run from the town's shore.

ESTABLISHMENT 3

Prairie Inn Neighbourhood Pub

7806 East Saanich Road, Saanichton
1-250-652-1575
Manager – Jamie Day
Services – wi-fi, wheelchair-accessible with wheel chair-accessible washrooms

Location

At the intersection of East Saanich Road and Mount Newton Cross-road. A bus exchange is located nearby.

What makes the Prairie Inn unique: history, period architecture and decor, haunted(?)

The Prairie Inn is like a contemporary time machine, its bones locked in a remembered past while the world has changed around it.
In 1859, William Simpson built the original Prairie Tavern in the young Saanichton community. There are references dating to 1873 to a Henry Simpson as owner of the tavern. In 1893 he built a new inn beside the old. It stands to this day, considerably modified on the inside but retaining vestiges, inside and out, of its passage through time. Over the years, the building remained the centre of a bustling little town, serving for a time as a general store and post office until, in 1974, it was reincarnated as a pub.

Sitting on the porch, with glass affording protection from the late season elements, it is easy to feel yourself transported back in time. Framed in clapboard, with wooden floors, the two-storey complex exudes western history. The interior blends warm reminders

of the past with a modern sports-bar section complete with pool table, TVs and sports memorabilia. The past has its place, too; comfortable side rooms are adorned with photos of the early pub, a stained-glass picture of the pub, a fireplace, prints, wall-mounted antique flintlocks dating from the early to mid-1800s, and a host of memorabilia that warms the richly wooded walls, offering a sense of age and intimacy. A family-friendly restaurant section allows all ages to experience the inn.

The pub's goal is to maintain a friendly feeling of safety and comfort for its many regulars, and there is a strong commitment to community, reflected in the numerous fundraisers run by the inn. As in the past, it remains a centre of the little community. For many years, the Prairie Inn operated a brew pub, but in the mid-1990s it was deemed too expensive to continue. In a nod to Island business the pub carries on tap craft beers by Victoria-based breweries Phillips, Hoyne, and Driftwood, complemented by Cobblestone stout. One claim to fame is that it served as a backdrop for the movie Poker Night, starring Ron Perlman of Hellboy fame.

There are some who claim spirits of the non-liquid kind also walk its halls. Perhaps history is less silent than the well-worn walls of the Prairie Inn.

Earning your beer

Within a short driving distance are the extensive hiking trails of John Dean Provincial Park, centred around Mount Newton, an area famed for its spring wildflowers. Check env.gov.bc.ca/bcparks/explore/park-pgs/john_dean or, for another access through Haldon Park, check johndeanpark/south-entrance-to-john-dean-park. Note that the park is closed to vehicle traffic from November to March.

Close by the pub is the Saanich Pioneers museum, housed in a log building (7910 Polo Park Crescent, 250-658-8347, saanichpioneersociety.org) .

ESTABLISHMENT 4

Brentwood Bay Pub

849 Verdier Avenue, Brentwood Bay
1-250-544-2079
Webpage – brentwoodbayresort.com
Services – wi-fi, wheelchair-accessible with wheelchair-accessible washrooms

Location
At the water end of Verdier Avenue, where one can catch the Brentwood Bay Ferry to Mill Bay. Served by B.C. Transit bus #81. Ample parking is available across the road from the pub.

What makes Brentwood Bay Pub unique: location, setting, architecture, views and history
The form may be ultra-modern, but the tradition is old.

Back in the 1930s, the likes of Bob Hope came to this area for the wondrous fishing and rustic setting, joined in later years by Pierre Elliot Trudeau. Here, workboats would load and disgorge residents of the village who worked across the bay at Bamberton Ocean Cement. The Mill Bay ferry (predating BC Ferries) was already plying the waters to Mill Bay, and the little fishing lodge and marina prospered. But times change, and the lodge fell into disrepair and bankruptcy despite its scenic setting and waterborne resources. That was when Dan Behune, who had long run a boutique Tudor-style B&B in Victoria, saw the promise and acted.

On May 27, 2004, a luxury boutique hotel, the Brentwood Bay Resort and Spa, complete with a stylish new pub, opened its doors. The pub's soaring full bank of windows frames a panoramic view of Brentwood Bay and the rising green mountains

beyond. Below, the marina still bobs with boat life, and the lodge rooms spread behind. This is an eye-catching setting made for quiet lingering and visual reflection or happy group gatherings.

The heavily wooded theme sports rich-hued Douglas fir beams, straight-grain fir veneered panelling, reclaimed wood for table tops, a warming hearth and an upper balcony. Outside, a heated patio with a fire pit lends air and scent to the scene. From bar to table, the seating is spacious and accommodating. A pervading sense of space and natural beauty radiates from the place.

The lodge and pub have drawn the Hollywood likes of Meg Ryan, Robert Redford, Adam Brody and Ellen Tyne Daly, while remaining broadly welcoming of regular folk. Also being drawn are Island-produced craft beers, including the offerings of Victoria breweries Hoyne, Phillips, and Driftwood, and the Cowichan Valley's Merridale Cider. In addition to the local brews, the pub has several taps that change seasonally.

As in the past, the marina lives on below, and in the parking lot a carving of an old sailor, who once stood amid the surroundings of the previous pub, still stands guard. The walls may change, but the watch remains.

Earning your beer

You can interact with Brentwood Bay's setting in a variety of simple and engaged ways. For a small cash fare you can hop aboard the Mill Bay ferry as a foot passenger and enjoy the 25-minute scenic cruise to the distant shore, drinking in the scenery and never knowing what you will spy in the greater bay's waters. (bcferries.com)
The marina has much of the sea to offer, be it by way of rentals (kayaks, canoes and paddleboards) or excursions. Take a water tour from here to the world-famed Butchart Gardens, where summer Saturdays end with a stunning fireworks display, or head underwater on a diving trip to see rich sea life, such as giant Pacific octopus, wolf eels, rare sea sponges, and more. Perhaps take an eco-tour on the marina's glass-domed excursion craft.

Perhaps consider the opportunity to hike the trails of nearby Gowlland Tod Provincial Park (env.gov.bc.ca/bcparks/explore/parkpgs/gowlland_tod/)

ESTABLISHMENT 5

Smugglers Cove Pub

2581 Penrhyn Street, Victoria

	1-250-477-2688
Webpage –	smugglerscovepub.com
Services –	wi-fi, wheelchair-accessible with wheelchair-accessible washrooms downstairs

Location

Penrhyn Street leads to Gyro Park, off of Cadboro Bay Road. Smugglers Cove Pub is tucked behind its ample parking lot, just to your right as you head toward the beach.

What makes Smugglers Cove Pub unique: setting, theme, location

Word has it Smugglers Cove Pub was constructed in 1980 in imitation of an original pub in Bath, England, where the first owner originated. If so, it comes by its English pub theme honestly and is a good fit for the seaside village of Cadboro Bay. It was called the Barley Mow Inn when it first came to life as a restaurant, which was followed by the name Cock and Bull. Present owner Brian Dunn gave it the current name when he took it over in 1996. Though Cadboro Bay was not known for smuggling, there is a Smugglers Cove at nearby Ten Mile Point.

The two-floor building, with an outdoor patio on the second level, maintains an English theme inside and out. The exterior features Tudor-style stucco and timber facing with peaked gables and a shake roof, while the inside is adorned with colourful stained-glass windows and historic photos of Cadboro Bay lining the walls. Sectioned off with banisters and a raised dais, the ample space offers bar, bench and table seating,

(photo courtesy Smugglers Cove Pub)

accommodating groups large and small. A high, vaulted ceiling in the central section lends a bit of "great hall" feel to the place. The outdoor deck is well sheltered under a sprawling awning. Priding itself on being a pub for the neighbourhood, it exudes a community feel. A local well-moneyed gent can be spotted sitting alongside a university student watching his beer budget, both in equal comfort. The staff have been here for pushing 20 years, and the combination makes for a true neighbourhood pub, where faces have names.

Priding itself on its menu and beverages, Smugglers lends its endorsement strongly to local craft breweries, carrying the products of Victoria breweries Phillips, Driftwood, and Hoyne. The majority of its taps are turned to local product, and there's a rotating tap for visiting beers. Special mention needs be made of the Guinness here, as the pub has, for three straight years, won Victoria's Best Guinness accolades. The English theme befits both village and seaside, and with it comes a sense that Smugglers Cove Pub is as natural a part of the village and community as the local coffee shop or grocery store.

Earning your beer
You need go no farther than Gyro Beach, right behind the pub, to find yourself entertained and occupied. The broad beach and sea vista are well suited to strolling, sea watching, photography, and so forth. Perhaps you'll get a glimpse of legendary "Caddy," the elusive sea serpent said to ply these waters. Explore the little village of Cadboro Bay, go for a walk around the neighbourhood, or venture farther afield to the nearby grounds of the University of Victoria. On these grounds is Mystic Vale. Here, where well-used trails wend through forest and along stream and pool, there are legends. That it was sacred to the First Nations people is a certainty, but what of the story that there was once a pure spring-water pool that lapped at the foot of a great maple tree—a tree said to be a god who protected the pool. Should it be cut down, the pool would vanish, or so the story went. Back in the 1860s there were tales that reflections in the pool could tell boys or girls who loved them and who they would eventually marry.

There is also the mysterious story of Julia Booth, who in 1868 was found dead at the pool, cause unknown. Food for thought while walking the forested halls. Twice a year, the village streets of Cadboro Bay are blocked off for festivals, during the Christmas Carolling event and a summer art festival in August. Take a bus to Cadboro Bay and spend a day at the seaside, with a brew to follow—just like a short holiday to England by the sea.

ESTABLISHMENT 6

Christie's Pub

1739 Fort Street, Victoria

1-250-598-5333
Webpage – christiespub.com
Services – wi-fi, wheelchair-accessible with wheelchair-accessible washrooms

Location
Along Fort Street, east of downtown Victoria.

What makes Christie's Pub unique: architecture, history, décor and hauntings (?)

The 1905 Rockaway Coupe horse-drawn carriage holding court at the entrance is a foot in the past of what is today's Christie's pub. It's a history not forgotten within the ornate walls of this Edwardian mansion.

Eldridge Christie built his home, "Sandolph," in 1898, in the style known as Queen Anne. The family lived there, building horse-drawn carriages on the site, until 1909. Seeing the writing on the wall with the advent of the automobile, Eldridge up and moved his family and business to Ashcroft, where he plied his trade building and repairing coaches for the famed BX Stage Line. The vintage Rockaway carriage, with its five seats and three drop-away windows, was one of the few hard-top carriages in Victoria at the time, the majority being soft-tops.

The home remained in the family until 1948, then drifted between owners and uses until, facing possible demolition, it was saved by a group of local businessmen. In 1986, it opened as Christie's Pub. One of its past incarnations was

as a nurses' residence, where, it turns out, present-day general manager Brock Carbery's mother once resided.

Restored to Edwardian style, the richly decorated interior glints with leaded and stained glass, dark-rose wainscotting and bar, soft carpeted floors, and ample windows. Accommodating up to 155 patrons, it has plenty of room for larger groups, as well as nooks and crannies for greater privacy. In addition to the three indoor sections, an all-season patio with heaters and an open fire pit helps to bring the outdoors in.

Of the 37 beers on tap, 80% are craft beers, with representation from local Victoria breweries Phillips, Vancouver Island, Driftwood, Lighthouse and Hoyne. Wheelchair-friendly Christie's also offers music every Saturday from 7:30 to 10:30 p.m. For those concerned about drinking and driving, the availability of good bus service is a plus. Ample parking is available.

And when the lights go out and everyone has gone home? There are things that go bump in the night. On at least one occasion, a staff member has been sent scurrying downstairs after feeling a ghostly tap on his shoulder. Others have spoken about strange noises emanating from the attic.

Mike, who has been tending the bar for over 26 years, believes the tales and is of the opinion that a young lad of about age 10 from the late 1800s roams the building.

Certainly, the age and history of this building, coupled with its period restoration, provides the setting for a restless or perhaps comforted soul.

Earning Your Beer
Put your feet to good use, and there is much to see in the neighbourhood. Willows Beach is a 15- to 20-minute walk, and reasonable strolls will take you to the Oak Bay Village on Fort Street, the gardens of Government House (home of the Lieutenant Governor of B.C.) (governor. vic.gov.au/government-house) and historic Craigdarroch Castle (the-castle.ca).

ESTABLISHMENT 7

The Beagle Pub

301 Cook Street, Victoria

	1-250-382-3301
Webpage –	beaglepub.ca
Services –	wi-fi, wheelchair-accessible with wheel chair-accessible washrooms

Location
At the corner of Oxford and Cook, in the heart of Victoria's Cook Street Village. Look for a free-standing wrought-iron clock.

What makes the Beagle unique: architecture, location, setting and theme

Cook Street Village is one of those places where the larger urban world leaves space for the legacy of a more communal time; it's a neighbourhood with the simple appeal of a world where people know each other and share a sense of belonging. This is fortunate for those living there and of visceral appeal for those visiting. The Beagle is as much a part of this urban oasis as breath is to lungs or salt to seawater. Born as the Oxford Arms in 1989, under the guiding hand of original owner Harry Lucas, and reflecting a British theme, it eventually was renamed the Flying Beagle. When the new, four-man ownership group took over in 2001, the Beagle ceased to fly and took on its present title.

Owning its corner like a ship's figurehead, the coat of arms sign (complete with rampant beagle and collared steed beside a shield with grapes and wheat sheaf, topped by a beer stein) thunders British. And the wrought-iron corner clock, readily visible to those awaiting company, would make Sherlock Holmes himself at ease. The patio, fenced in

glass, allows patrons to take in the passing parade of people strolling under the shade of trees that line Oxford Street. In spring and summer, the flower-bedecked exterior of the pub can't fail to garner notice. The visual appeal of the Beagle's exterior wasn't lost on well-known Victoria artist Robert Amos, whose gallery of Cook Street Village paintings (robertamos. com) includes two seasonal Beagle frames. The lively, single-level venue welcomes you with sectioned-off niches, a raised dais and seating ranging from bar to table to bench, offering space for groups large and small. The stained-glass dome overhead, which once owned the centre of the pub and had a forest of glasses hanging from its bowl, has found a new place of honour near the bar.

Carrying 35 beers and cider on tap, the Beagle prides itself on offering a wide variety of craft brewery suds. Victoria's own Hoyne, Phillips, Driftwood, Vancouver Island, and Lighthouse products are available, as are the brews of Salt Spring Island Brewery and the famed Guinness. All but three taps are devoted to B.C. craft products. Neil Baird, one of the owners, has known the pub since its opening days and is a long-time Victorian. He noted the unique neighbourliness of the Beagle, a place where a couple in their 90s can comfortably sit down next to a long-haired student and a group catching a game on the screen above. This is very much a place frequented on foot and part of everyday life in the village. Like the old pubs of English villages, the Beagle is a defining element of Cook Street Village.

Earning your beer
Best to don your walking shoes, for there's lots to see in the neighbourhood. Beacon Hill Park is a couple of easy blocks away and faces the Dallas Road path, which opens up stunning sea vistas all the way to the Olympic Range in Washington and gives pups (including regular but not flying beagles) the opportunity to roam about unleashed. The sea is alive with activity, from whale tour boats to paragliders, naval vessels, cruise ships and the ever-popular sea life, when it chooses to make itself visible.

For history buffs, historic Ross Bay Cemetery is nearby. Among its famed "residents" are the likes of pioneer Governor James Douglas (the inspiration for a Hollywood movie if ever there was one) and Hockey Hall of Fame brothers Lester and Frank Patrick (Lester won the Stanley Cup for Victoria in 1925). Its shaded lawns and forest cover make it as cool and refreshing on a summer's day as it is eerie when the sun flees and darkness rolls in. It is easy to see why there are many who see this graveyard as a place of hauntings.

The Moss Street Market (mossstreetmarket.com) runs on Saturdays, May to October, and is within a few blocks of the Beagle. You can easily spend many an informative hour just wandering the neighbourhood and strolling the pedestrian-friendly, chestnut-lined sidewalks of the village itself. (cookstreetvillage.ca)

ESTABLISHMENT 8

The Penny Farthing Public House

2228 Oak Bay Ave., Victoria
1-250-370-9008
Webpage – pennyfarthingpub.com
Services – wi-fi, wheelchair-accessible with wheel chair-accessible washrooms

Location
On Oak Bay Avenue in the heart of Oak Bay Village

What makes the Penny Farthing unique: setting, architecture, decor, theme

It began with a parade in 1997.

Businessman Matt MacNeil, with a pub pedigree from Alberta and B.C., had recently moved to Victoria and was enjoying the annual Oak Bay Tea Party Parade, led for the 55th time by local legend Jack Leonard on his superbly home-built penny-farthing bicycle. Matt decided there and then that his planned local pub would carry the name Penny Farthing. Matt and Jack became friends, and that original bike now holds centre court in the pub of the same name.

The bike, circa 1870s, takes its name from the image of the English penny, a large, heavy, round coin, and the farthing, a small, light coin, set together in bike form. In 2001, the new pub opened its majestic etched-glass and wood doors to the public. It has since become an integral part of the Oak Bay Village scene. Entering, you face a grand staircase overseen by Jack's penny-farthing.

Designed by Matt MacNeil

himself, as were his other two pubs, the Irish Times and the Bard and Banker, the Penny Farthing incorporates a rich heritage of English decor and memorabilia. With two floors and a year-round heated patio, there is ample room for the throngs, while maintaining a sense of intimate space. There's room here for groups of one to 150. Seating in side rooms, booths, at the bar and at tables accommodates groups large and small, allowing for the enjoyment of music as well as quieter conversation not far away. Redwood hues frame the warm, carpeted floors, below high ceilings sparkling with light and glass. It seems a new space opens up around each corner, and patrons can find intimate spots in little libraries, cubbyholes, sofa niches and fireplace-centred rooms akin to the comforts of home.

Historic and English-themed pictures and memorabilia adorn walls illuminated by a wealth of wall and post lamps, accentuated by sparkling chandeliers. Above the wainscotting, walls are decorated in colourful wallpaper, and the solid wood bar is artistically embossed. The stunning stained glass was produced by renowned artist Irene Gemmeel of Dublin. You'll find your eyes awash with things to see and ambience to drink in.

The Penny Farthing prides itself on serving on tap 12 beers produced within the immediate Victoria area, a testament to the craft brewing industry of Victoria represented by the Hoyne, Driftwood, Lighthouse, and Phillips breweries. Pride extends to the pouring of the perfect Guinness, instructions for which are included on the pub's website. Of the total 33 taps, eight are rotating and have carried products from the Townsite (Powell River) and Category 12 (Saanichton) breweries. Topping it off are four ciders on tap.

Where once there was a bit of controversy about the Penny Farthing, today it's well accepted, and perhaps no more so than in the section known as Platform 9 ¾, an homage to Harry Potter. Like clockwork, every day at 2 p.m. a few of the locals turn up to socialize in their assigned pub niche—named to honour one of their daughters and her affinity for the wizarding books. Jack Leonard may be gone now, but his Penny Farthing lives on in spirit and body.

<u>Earning your beer</u>
Oak Bay Village, spread along Oak Bay Avenue, has loads of shops and galleries to explore and every year is the venue for the Oak Bay Tea Party Parade (oakbayteaparty.com), led by Mrs. & Mrs. Tweedie (a nod to the famed Britishness of Oak Bay), which celebrated its 56th birthday in 2018. It is a healthy walk to Willows Beach and the enjoyment of the seaside.

ESTABLISHMENT 9

Moon Under Water

350B Bay Street, Victoria

	1-250-380-0706
Webpage –	moonunderwater.ca
Services –	wi-fi, wheelchair-accessible with wheelchair-accessible washrooms

<u>Location</u>
Keep an eye out on your right while heading for the Point Ellice Bridge from downtown Victoria along Bay Street. Lots of parking.

<u>What makes the Moon Under Water unique:</u> a storied name, brew pub, dog beer, a brewmasters' pub, and canine mascot Brew.
Crossing the threshold of what looks like a simple warehouse exterior already gives a suggestion of what to expect. Spacious and high-ceilinged, this is a brewery accommodating a pub. It may have little in common with most pubs, but then, this is not most pubs. This is a place where brewmasters congregate, and mascot Brew is a recognized Victoria personality. The Moon was only a year old when the new owners took over on Sept. 1, 2012, and began charting their own course. Brew, a multiracial breed affectionately termed a "short-haired handsome" is the face of the operation.

It is hard to beat the name, which was drawn from an item in the Manchester Evening Standard (Evening News) on Feb. 9, 1946, titled The Moon Under Water, by famed author George Orwell. The article described Orwell's fictional idea of his perfect pub.

In addition to their own 14 brew options, including Creepy Uncle Dunkel, Potts Pils, Tranquility IPA, Light Side of the Moon, and Hip as Funk Farmhouse IPA, there is the seasonal Dark Side of the Moon (stout) on tap. The pub also carries guest beers from breweries such as Salt Spring, Phillips, and Powell River's Townsite, to name a few. A unique feature is the rotating taps, which are switched to respected Canadian and international beers selected by the brewmaster.

And the pub has not forgotten Brew; it produces three differently flavoured "dog beers."

Alcohol-free, non-carbonated, and hops-free, the pup brews are rich in glucosamine (for joints) and fish oils for glossy fur. The brew's fame is making its way up the Island. The pub sports a brewmasters wall of fame, where photos of known and respected brewmasters, both local and international, are featured. Pride is taken in being a pub where brewmasters from the varying Island breweries gather socially.

For aficionados, the pub offers tours and tastings, as it is on the cruise ship city-excursion schedule. You can also order a sampler flight of their products so as to savour them side by side. At the time of writing there were plans to open a new distillery next door, to include a tasting room for gin, vodka, whiskey and liquors.

The setting is open, spacious, and modern, with seating accommodating everyone from individuals to larger groups. One section is centred around a fireplace, cozy and separate. Check out the unique anteroom floored entirely with pennies in an artistic arrangement. The atmosphere is welcoming, whether you are ending a day spent at the construction site or a camera-toting tourist.

But then, you would expect that from a place with a contented dog mascot (after all—three flavoured dog beers!). We know how welcoming dogs are.

Earning your beer

The Songhees Trail is just across the Point Ellice Bridge and connects you to other paved trails skirting the greater Victoria Harbour and hinterlands. Bike, hike, go inline skating, run, whatever—there is a more than a day of play to enjoy here before a cool brew. Afterward, should you need it, the downtown bus service is good, and you can even leave your car at the Moon Under Water pub overnight. Cards are available with information on alternatives for transport home. The pub's growing appeal is reflected in its inclusion on Victoria excursions for cruise ship passengers and its popularity with cyclists. As it's near Victoria's inner harbour and downtown, there is so much to see and do in the area that it's worthwhile to do a little advance planning. Check out tourismvictoria.com.

Garrick's Head Pub

69 Bastion Square, Victoria

	1-250-384-6835
Webpage –	garrickshead.com
Services –	wi-fi, wheelchair-accessible with wheel chair-accessible washrooms

Location
Smack dab at Bastion Square, Victoria.

What makes the Garrick's Head unique: history, location, setting, architecture, a huge range of beer on tap, hauntings (?)

People have been hanging around the drinking establishment at this location since 1867. Quite literally. Word is, the famous Hanging Judge, Matthew Begbie, used to bring the condemned here for their last meal and drink before facing the gallows in Bastion Square.

The pub, which greets patrons with a keg hanging over the front door, butts up against the Bedford Regency Hotel, with which it is associated. The hotel is housed in the 1910 Hibben-Bone building, both venues having a long association with historic Victoria. Recorded as having opened on Dec. 31, 1867, Garrick's Head is one of the oldest English pubs in Canada. Legend has it that it's haunted by the ghost of former owner Michael Powers, mysteriously murdered over a century ago,

sometimes seen standing by the wood-burning fireplace—the only one still functioning in downtown Victoria—on a chilly winter's evening.

Begbie would have a tough time choosing a beer if he came back today. Garrick's Head has an array of 55 taps incorporating all of Victoria's craft beers, save for some from the brewpubs, plus a huge list of other craft beers. Add to this the 50 taps at its sister pub (The Churchill), and you have enough for a destination sampling holiday. Rotating taps add to the appeal for aficionados. Check out garrickshead.com for more information.

With its high ceiling and many windows, the pub exudes an almost outdoor feel. Brick walls meet wood floors, and the polished 44-foot bar is topped with quilted maple and stained birch. The back section, with cozy, subdued lighting, is warmed by the brick fireplace overseen by a stoic deer's head. Seating, from bench to bar to table and chairs, is spread liberally, allowing plenty of space. Large windows encourage people-watching in Bastion Square, a pastime accentuated on the outdoor patio.
Vibrant and alive, both pub and square mark a stark contrast to the somber hosting of the condemned by the Hanging Judge, so many years past.

Earning your beer
Like other unique pubs in the core of old Victoria, Garrick's Head is central to all the popular sights for visitors: shopping, the provincial Parliament Buildings, Empress Hotel, harbour, the Royal British Columbia Museum, and more. It is also, along with its neighbour the Irish Times, right at Bastion Square. This pedestrian mall, which fronts on the B.C. Maritime Museum, is the site of many ongoing events, including the summer public markets. From May to September the public market, celebrating its 23rd year in 2018, runs from 11 a.m. to 5:30 p.m. Thursday through Saturday and 10 a.m. to 4:30 p.m. Sundays. It offers entertainment as well as arts and crafts.

As for getting a bit of exercise, healthy waterside walks can take you around the harbour and the Empress all the way out to Fisherman's Wharf. Going the other way, an equally frisky trek takes you over the Johnson Street Bridge and all the way to West Bay.
Truth is, in downtown Victoria there is much more to do than you can cover in one visit.

ESTABLISHMENT 11

The Irish Times Public House

1200 Government Street, Victoria
1-250-383-7775
Webpage –   irishtimespub.ca
Services –   wi-fi, wheelchair-accessible with wheelchair-accessible washrooms (elevator)

Location
On Government Street by Bastion Square

What makes the Irish Times unique: history, location, decor, theme
Born of stone and style in 1894, the Irish Times Public House began life as the chateau-styled Bank of Montreal. The master of its creation was renowned architect Francis Mawson Rattenbury, who also designed the B.C. Parliament Buildings and the Empress Hotel. His was a story whose end would befit an Agatha Christie murder mystery, and it is deeply embedded in the architectural history of Victoria.

The asymmetrical four-storey steel and stone edifice has a castle-like appearance complete with gargoyles, sloped roofline, pillars, cornices and crenellated corners. Meant to inspire awe and confidence in 1894, it continues to do so.

(photo courtesy Irish Times)

When Matt MacNeil ventured into creating the Irish Times he discovered both Rattenbury's original design sketches for the bank and its ornate ceiling, which had been hidden over the years. After re-exposing the original ceiling, he had an artist spend six months restoring it. Renovations also revealed the underground trolley system that once provided a secure connection to other banks and pipes from the old Victoria Steam Company that were used to heat downtown buildings until the 1960s.

The two interior pub levels, joined by staircases fitted with wrought-iron banisters, house many niches, cubbyholes, library rooms, and secluded fireplace-centred spaces—a host of venues for group and couple gatherings. The impression is rather like Doctor Who's "bigger on the inside than the outside" Tardis. Various imported materials and art pieces were installed, including stained and etched glass by famed Dublin artist Irene Gemmeel, adding to the effect of authenticity that hits the moment you pass through the regal doors. Everywhere you look, there is light and appealing features: radiant chandeliers, historic photos of famed Irish writers, ornate bars, singularly attractive fireplaces, arched windows. This is as much a gallery of artistry as a welcoming pub, offering something and somewhere for everybody.

Inside, the pub has 190 seats, with a further 80 on the outdoor patios opening on Bastion Square and Government Street. The upper-floor mezzanine tops out at 100 seats, while the "McCarthy Snug" holds 16 and the "O'Hagan's Snug" offers cozy surroundings for up to 10.

Music runs seven nights a week, with no cover charge, and the 44 taps dispense 16 local craft beers, nine Vancouver beers and four ciders. All of the Irish beers, including Guinness, are directly imported from Ireland. Add to this the reputedly largest selection of Irish whiskey in Canada, and you have more than enough choices to endorse numerous visits. Rattenbury himself would be proud to see what has become of his inspirational creation.

Yet his tale ended poorly. Some years after leaving his wife of 25 years for 27-year-old Kamloops-born Alma Pakenham (nee Clarke), he was found dead in his parlour in Bournemouth, England, on March 23, 1935—the victim of repeated hammer blows to the head from Alma's 18-year-old chauffeur and lover. At the time he was 68, with his career fading, and was suffering financial problems. Despite his former fame, he was buried in Bournemouth in a grave that remained unmarked until a family friend installed a stone in 2007. The chauffeur served seven years of a life sentence, and Alma committed suicide three days after her acquittal on charges of complicity in the crime, on June 4, 1935, by stabbing herself and jumping into the river. Drama fit for the stage.

From great fame and fortune Rattenbury may have fallen, but his works, of which the Irish Times is one, remain very much alive.

Earning your beer

Thanks to its site in the heart of old Victoria, activities near the Irish Times are seemingly endless, and a visit to the tourist information centre will give you loads of options. Perhaps one option would be a walk to survey the Rattenbury legacy. A short stroll down Government Street brings you to both the Empress Hotel (1903) and the B.C. Parliament Buildings (1893). Guided tours or walkabouts can easily eat up a day of exploring. The Rattenbury legacy is deep in Victoria and the province, though many a building has been lost to the ravages of time. A provincial tour of his courthouses alone would take you to Nelson, Revelstoke, Vancouver, and Nanaimo.

Check out the tourist information centre at Humboldt and Government Street, overlooking the inner harbour. (tourismvictoria.com)

ESTABLISHMENT 12

The Churchill

1140 Government Street

	1-250-384-6835
Webpage –	thechurchill.ca
Services –	wi-fi, wheelchair-accessible with wheelchair-accessible washrooms

<u>Location</u>
On Government Street just below Bastion Square.

<u>What makes the Churchill unique:</u> Over fifty taps and history
Like the mouse that roared, the Churchill is proof you shouldn't be quick to judge on size. Tucked away in a street frontage corner of the Bedford Regency Hotel complex (once the Churchill Hotel of heritage fame), which also houses the Garrick's Head, the Churchill seems to expand and lengthen into a wood-decorated pub with a capacity of 90 patrons.

Its namesake pub was originally downstairs and suffered infamy from the 1940s to the 1970s as the haunt of bikers, ruffians and ladies of the night. There are stories of bikers riding their Harleys down the stairs and up to the bar.

Reopened upstairs in 2014, it has rebuilt its reputation on more positive terms, sharing fame with the Garrick's Head for its abundance of taps and beer options. Fully 50 taps represent craft beers, including nine rotating ones that wheel through a host of different products in the course of a day. It is impossible to sample them

all, even with the option of four-glass flights; there is just too much change and variety. All the local brewery names are there: Phillips, Vancouver Island, Hoyne, Driftwood, Lighthouse, Moon, Category 12, and Longwood of Nanaimo, to name but a few. They also carry a variety of stouts, including Guinness.

In addition, the pub offers 60 whiskeys and a specialty cocktail list famed for its individuality and originality. Its polished, 46-foot black walnut bar, trimmed in zebra wood, is lined with chairs, but there are also booths and a big, circular communal table for groups. As it's blessed with a number of big-screen TVs, it is a surprise to find sports do not provide the viewing content here. Instead the screens offer, in black and white, still photos or old movies. It's a party pleaser.
So, next time you think to judge a book by its cover, especially an old cover, think again. The Churchill is back, and worth a visit.

Earning Your Beer
You can't go wrong with a double-decker Victoria sightseeing tour, especially those that offer hop-on/hop-off options. Check out hellobc.com/victoria/things-to-do/arts-culture-history/historic-heritage-sites.aspx for information on bus tours and many other options.

ESTABLISHMENT 13

The Bard and Banker Public House

1022 Government Street, Victoria

Webpage –
Services –

1-250-953-9993
bardandbanker.com
wi-fi, wheelchair-accessible with wheel
chair-accessible washrooms

Location
At intersection of Government and Fort streets

What makes the Bard and Banker unique: history, architecture, decor, location, haunting (?)

What words of later fame were spoken within the walls of this place? If eras are remembered in stone and glass, so are those who spent time therein.

The Bard and Banker aptly draws its name from the brief stint that Robert Service, the great Klondike Poet (internal.org/Robert_W_Service), spent at the building, then a Canadian Bank of Commerce branch during the years 1903–1904. Built in 1883, the building remained a bank until 1988, followed by an interlude of 20 years as a Christmas shop before reopening as a Scottish pub in 2008.

Robert Service, then on the cusp of his thirties, patrolled these floors and took to sleeping in the vault, where one might suspect he took advantage of the solitude to intone verses he was contemplating. His memory is honoured in the pub name, the Vault niche, where perhaps echoes of those verses still vibrate, and in the Service 1904 beer on tap, crafted by Phillips Brewery. Historic photos and mementoes of the bard adorn walls and crannies.

Another name honoured on these walls is that of Victoria Cross recipient James Cleland Richardson. At the tender age of 20, this young bagpiper, on Oct. 8, 1916—the Battle of the Somme—inspired his companions of the 16th Infantry Division of the Canadian Expeditionary Force to a successful assault on the German lines, by striding before the trenches in full view of the enemy, pipes a-wailing. Surviving the assault, he later returned to the field of action to seek his lost pipes—and was never seen again. Seven years later his pipes were found; his body never was. Vancouver Island's Piper's Pale Ale honours his memory.

And now these walls ring to the sounds of social gatherings, amid a setting as vibrant as a memorial as it is in its decor. As with the Irish Times and the Penny Farthing, owner Matt MacNeil has gone to great lengths to design the layout and style of this historic themed edifice. He brought in or commissioned period-appropriate chandeliers, wood panelling and wainscotting, while incorporating historic glass, wood and marble elements remaining from the building's bank days. Of singular note are the banisters of the upper deck, wrought from the original railing that adorned the bank's peak, in which are incorporated the pub's crest of thistle, rose and shamrock.

As with Matt's other pubs, the artistic glass works of Irish artist Irene Gemmeel flavour the walls and windows. Niches, cubbyholes, bar seating, fireplace-centred rooms, library-themed sections and two outdoor patios (the upper of which offers a view of the harbour) can accommodate throngs in boisterous communalism as well as couples seeking intimate conversation. Though heavily embellished with attractions that present a feast for the eyes, its high ceilings, open two-level design, clutch of anterooms and "snugs" and sparkling lighting imbue the pub with a sense of spaciousness.

The pub carries 26 beers on tap. The tilt to Victoria craft breweries is reflected in the fact that 17 of the taps are devoted to local brews, including the offerings of Victoria's Phillips, Lighthouse, and Hoyne breweries. This is complemented by four taps offering ciders and one the cherished Guinness.

Live music, free of cover charge, is provided seven days a week; a baby grand piano adds to the potential for musical scope. As if these walls didn't hold enough secrets, it's rumoured that the ghost of an unknown lady walks the second floor of the building, her presence occasionally glimpsed at the window. The makings of a Service poem, I should think.

Earning your beer

You can eat up the greater part of a day exploring the offerings of pedestrian-friendly Government Street and old Chinatown before nipping in for a brew. With so much to see and do, it is worth a trip in person or by internet to the Victoria tourism office at Humboldt and Government Streets (tourismvictoria.com).

(photo courtesy Smuggers Cove Pub)

ESTABLISHMENT 14

Canoe Brew Pub & Marina

450 Swift Street, Victoria

Webpage –
Services –

1-250-361-1940
canoebrewpub.com
wi-fi, wheelchair-accessible with wheel
chair-accessible washrooms

Location
Waterside, one block north of the Johnson Street Bridge, off of Store Street. There is parking on site, and buses run nearby.

What makes the Canoe Brew Pub unique: history, decor, architecture, location, setting, and it's a brew pub
The Gorge waterfront has known great changes since the 1990s. Its rough-edged industrial face has seen the benefits of a makeover, and nowhere is this more apparent than the frog-into-prince story of the Canoe Brew Pub and Marina.

What was once a coal-fired power plant feeding the needs of upstart Victoria in the late 1800s is now a renovated brewpub as appealing on the exterior as it is compelling when you enter the door. Born in 1894 of brick and steel, the building was the stuff of a gritty industry not given to paint and polish. But it did not give up all of the past in becoming the prince of today. The bricks and bones of the original remain, but cleaned up, bathed in natural light, and accentuated with wood, rails and atmosphere.

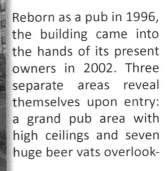

Reborn as a pub in 1996, the building came into the hands of its present owners in 2002. Three separate areas reveal themselves upon entry: a grand pub area with high ceilings and seven huge beer vats overlook-

ing the expansive bar; a smaller lounge area with pool table and its own bar and fireplace; plus an upstairs loft restaurant accommodating families. The welcoming foyer is brightly illuminated with natural light and the sparkle of ornate chandeliers. Outside, patio seating accommodates fully 250 patrons, with a view of the dynamic life of the Gorge Waterway and the ever-changing face of the area.

Its decor proves that functionality doesn't preclude beauty, as the huge cedar-beam and steel seismic reinforcements, despite their purpose, are nonetheless attractive.

And this is a brew pub, part of the flourishing craft-beer community that is earning acclaim and patronage in Victoria.

The four signature beers are handcrafted in small batches, using only the finest malted barley, hops, yeast and water. They hover in the 5% alcohol range and are brewed under the strict rules of the Bavarian Purity Law of 1516. You can savour the taste of all four with the purchase of a flight sampler combination. It's well worth the experience if you think there is little difference between brews. To this, add the company's five seasonal beers, which include the award-winning Bavarian Copper Bock.

Pride is taken not only in the menu offerings but also in support for local farmers, seasonal use of organics, and attention to serving sustainably harvested meat and seafood.

Local live music is offered Thursday, Friday, and Saturday, and among the special events celebrated here are the Winter Brau, hosting other Victoria craft breweries, and the summer solstice kickoff. Outside, the waters of the Gorge and Inner Harbour beckon. Though the marina is not for public use, there is space for kayakers and canoeists to haul their craft ashore, to dine and imbibe at the outdoor patio. And so, craft beer in hand, the prince can relax in the shadow of his hard-working past and tip his glass to the legacy of the frog.

Earning your beer
Kayakers and canoeists can enjoy the waters of the harbour and Gorge, with more than a day's worth of exploring to keep body and mind active. Those inclined to less intimacy with the water can opt for water taxi or harbour cruises that put in and out from the Canoe Brew Pub marina and connect widely throughout the watercourse. You can even use the water taxis to enjoy a responsible pub crawl, as a host of pubs are close by, or, in the case of Spinnakers and the Canoe Brew Pub, have their own nearby stops.

Victoria's renowned Chinatown is a only couple of blocks away, and the MacPherson theatre next to that.

ESTABLISHMENT 15

The Sticky Wicket

919 Douglas Street, Victoria
　　　　　　　　1-250-383-7137
Webpage –　　　strathconahotel.com
Services-　　　　wi-fi

<u>Location</u>
At Douglas and Courtenay, near the Empress Hotel complex

<u>What makes the Sticky Wicket unique:</u> architecture, decor, location, theme, history and range of entertainment and service

The Sticky Wicket strikes the eye as so inherently Victoria, British Columbia, that it feels in sympathetic heartbeat with the proud Empress Hotel and the Parliament Buildings. Its stately frontage, with many windows and flowers, gives but a hint of what's inside.
Housed within the historic confines of the Strathcona Hotel, it shares space with the hotel, the upper-floor outdoor Surf Club (complete with sand volleyball court), a nightclub, restaurant, and the wild Big Bad John's bar, with its sawdust floor, Appalachian theme, and name recalling founder John Olson. In total, the complex holds up to 1,600 people!

It was born in 1913 as neither pub nor hotel, but as the Empress Building, local headquarters of the Royal Air Force until 1918. In 1989, Olson took on a major renovation of the property and, together with architect J.C. Scott, designed the complex it was to become. Concepts were generated during a trip to England, where John got the idea of a cricket theme. These many years later, the theme

persists, and the family carries on the tradition. The Strathcona Hotel garnered an A-class liquor licence in 1954, the first in Victoria, and in 1989 opened the Sticky Wicket Pub.

The theme is represented throughout the pub in the form of cricket regalia (bats, wickets and such) plus lots of cricket photos, both local and international. Fittingly, the pub sponsors a local cricket team and often hosts visiting sides. The walls of the Wenman Room are adorned with historic photos of a famed cricketer, Victoria's own Reg Wenman, who starred locally and internationally, earning a place in the Greater Victoria Sports Hall of Fame for his 50-year career. Some credit him as the greatest cricketer in Canadian history.

There is much to gaze upon within these rich wood walls: memorabilia, fine custom-made mirrors imported from England, fireplaces, antique chandeliers, leaded glass, antique panelling, and the stunning glass works at the pub's entrance. Of special note is a large, three-dimensional sports-themed wall mural incorporating gloves, balls, saddles, oars, and more, all adhering to the green body of a pool table.
An air of welcoming opulence immediately captures your eye.
Of the 40 beers on tap, Victoria's rich craft-brew community is represented by Vancouver Island, Hoyne, Philllips, Driftwood, and Lighthouse breweries, as well as the elixirs of Salt Spring Island Brewery. Topping it off is Guinness on tap.
Bar and table seating comfortably accommodates groups large and small, and the many window seats offer a view of the busy world passing outside. A huge games room provides darts, pool, and sports on the screen.

Once a year, the pub opens up for a beer fest, inviting all the Island breweries and the interested public. This is no small attraction, in light of the growing number of Island and area craft breweries and the acclaim they're receiving, both popular and professional. The event speaks to an impressive level of camaraderie and respect among Victoria's brewmasters and their teams.
It shouldn't be forgotten that the Sticky Wicket is just one part of the Strathcona's offerings, especially since its family restaurant gives all ages a chance to share in the experience. It all feels unmistakably Victoria—proof you can keep an eye on the present and a classy foot in the past.

Earning your beer

From the Sticky Wicket you are a short walk from Victoria's sprawling Beacon Hill Park, at once both manicured and wildly wind-blown.
Make your way to the sea cliff's edge to watch paragliders hanging
in the wind, happy leash-free dogs cavorting in their fenceless park,
whale-watch cruises flying out to sea, and the Coho ferry plying the
waters to Port Angeles, Wash., at the feet of the mighty Olympic
Range, which owns the horizon. There are trails and ponds, glades
and gardens, viewpoints and seascapes, plus a seaside walk that can
take up your entire day and leave more to spare. (beaconhillpark.ca)

Even closer is the stately Empress Hotel (fairmont.com/empress-vic-
toria), the renowned B.C. Provincial Museum (royalbcmuseum.bc.ca),
heritage buildings from Victoria's earliest fur-trade days and much
more. It is worth the time to visit the nearby tourist information centre and plan your downtown visit. There's more to do and see than a
day's visit can accommodate.

ESTABLISHMENT 16

The Bent Mast Restaurant

512 Simcoe Street, Victoria

1-250-383-6000

Webpage – bentmast.ca

Services- wi-fi

Location
In the heart of James Bay village, where Toronto and Simcoe streets converge onto Menzies. Bus service is good, via Beacon Hill bus #3, #27 and #28.

What makes the Bent Mast unique: history, location, setting, architecture, family-friendly, and hauntings (?)

An aura rests over this portal to the past, an aura thick with the journeys of many lives and their legacy in substance and atmosphere. It is a place to absorb, as much as see.

To the certain dismay of John Chandler, an accountant with the Hudson's Bay Company who built the house in 1884, his wife, Lizzie, preferred to live elsewhere. And so this fine, substantial edifice began its history of many owners. For long years it stood as a private home, the world slowly changing around it. From the 1930s, it embraced other uses: a rooming house, a residence for wives of sailors at sea during the war, a brothel, a student residence, an erotic gallery, and four different restaurant incarnations, before landing in the hands of new management in 1995.

Sailing folk, they erected a mast in front of the restaurant while still contemplating a name for their establishment. A friend commented on the mast being bent, by racing standards, and the unique name of the restaurant was born. The Bent Mast came under new ownership in 2015.

The two-storey building still bears traces of old elegance in its pillared entrance, high ceilings with ornate chandelier bases, molded cornices, high windows, fireplaces, stained glass and stairway made of woods imported from California. In one dining area, a section of the interior wall framing has been left exposed to reveal the cross-patterned framing used to earthquake-proof buildings back in the day. A two-tiered patio at the front is fenced low enough to allow for easy people-watching.

The interior flavour is one of casual comfort, showing the lady's age while yet favouring her attractions. Eclectic art adorns the walls, with a most compelling piece staring down upon you as you ascend the stairs to the restrooms.

And there are other eyes, perhaps. Numerous spirits are reputed to favour these walls, each taking up their own spots in the building. Downstairs resides the grouchy old man who likes to move things around. The main stairs are the abode of a couple of happy children who have been known to make themselves visible to children but otherwise annoy adults with their noisy ramblings. The top floor is home to a nice older woman thought to be the spirit of an elderly lady who died of injuries sustained in a robbery just outside the building.

Then there is the rude gentleman in the red fedora. Add to these entities bent on flipping items around, and you have a rather spirited atmosphere. The Bent Mast philosophy is to let the permanent residents have their space, and all co-exist quite well.

A popular local gathering place, the pub offers board games and live music on Thursdays (in the quiet, background folk-rock vein), and, as a family-friendly restaurant, lets the little folk share in the experience.

The Bent Mast owns 14 taps, all favouring local products, including the offerings of Phillips, Vancouver Island, Driftwood, Hoyne, and Lighthouse Breweries of Victoria. A homey focal point of James Bay Village for many a year, the Bent Mast draws its share of permanent residents and local patrons to enhance the welcome.

Earning your beer

On foot alone, there is much to see and do around the Bent Mast, including just walking around the neighbourhood to see the many heritage homes, including the onetime residence of famed artist Emily Carr (now a museum). But a few blocks away is sea-girded Dallas Road and Ogden Point, with its long breakwater pushing a nose into the sea alongside the cruise ship berths. Winding through the tended parkland is a coastal trail along the length of Dallas Road to Beacon Hill Park and beyond.

If you catch the right moment, you will find hobbyists with their radio-controlled model boats plying the sailing pond, with tugs, sailboats, submarines and more. Fisherman's Wharf is nearby, with its docked houseboats, food services, harbour ferries and entourage of ever-hungry harbour seals providing ongoing entertainment.

And if you want to experience the paranormal, consider Victoria's Ghostly Walks walking tours. (discoverthepast.com)

ESTABLISHMENT 17

Spinnakers Gastro Brewpub

308 Catherine Street, Victoria
                                1-250-386-2739
Webpage –   spinnakers.com
Services –   wi-fi, wheelchair-accessible with
                               wheelchair-accessible washrooms

Location

On Catherine Street, overlooking the harbour and kitty-corner to the development going on around the old Esquimalt & Nanaimo Railway roundhouse. Parking is available on the street and in a dedicated lot. Well-serviced by bus, with the Admirals Walk/Western Exchange Bus (#25) connecting with Yates Street downtown every 30 minutes (bc-transit.com/regions/vic).

The Victoria Harbour Ferry Songhees dock is only half a kilometre away, providing another relaxing and scenic connection to downtown Victoria (victoriaharbourferry.com).

What makes Spinnakers unique: view, location, history, setting, and it's a brew pub.

It was 1984 when Spinnakers caught the first gusts of the brew pub winds blowing across Canada. Though it claims the distinction of being the first brew pub in the country, it has not allowed itself to become a footnote in history.

Gusts of a different kind blew in a major fire in November 2016, from which the phoenix has arisen.

Since that event, Spinnakers has added a res-

(photo courtesy Spinnakers)

taurant, provisions store (carrying items such as artisan chocolates, homemade baked goods, Spinnakers malt vinegar and more) and heritage guest home (a restored 1884 residence), among other features, to its brew pub operation. The pub occupies the second floor of the scenically positioned lodge-like edifice, which gazes out to Victoria's busy harbour.

The comfortably worn wood interior has high ceilings and is filled with natural light from its many windows, overlooking lawn and water. Seating, from bar to table to bench, accommodates a good number of people, with partitioning to give groups separate space. Historic photos, including one of the old Goldstream Hotel, dot the walls, accompanied in places by model sailing ships. A pool table provides for entertainment, and the heated outdoor deck, guarded from the rain by transparent protection, gives fuller access to views across the busy harbour to the looming Olympic Range beyond.

Spinnakers has been involved in the farm-to-table movement, along with 35 local farms, since the early '90s, a fact reflected in its seasonally inspired menu items.

For beer aficionados, this is heaven. Over 30 brews are available at varying times, with such unique quaffs as Pumpkin Porter, Raspberry Ale, Swiftsure India Session Ale, Tour de Victoria Kolsch, Jamieson's Scottish Ale, Roundhouse Red, Sooke Plum Ale and, in answer to Guinness, Titanic and Irish stouts, to name but a few of the unique and storied beers available, all rich in European heritage and purity. Every Tuesday sees a rotating guest beer offered on tap. Spinnakers prides itself on providing Victoria's largest selection of traditional brews, owning an inventory of over 100 barrels, and is now playing around with barrel-aged beer as well as sours and lambic styles. For greater detail, check out the website.

When Spinnakers first came into being, the area about it was well-worn and industrial, focussed on the large roundhouse. Much has changed and is changing in the area, and Spinnakers is a pivotal part of that redefinition.

Sitting on the patio, with the wind in your sails and a fine Spinnakers brew in hand as you gaze upon a view fit for a king, it's easy to see why people keep coming back.

Earning your beer

You can easily earn your beer just getting here, as the Songhees Walkway passes just below Spinnakers, just 20 minutes from the Blue Bridge on Johnson Street. Allow yourself extra time to push on farther, to the trail's end at West Bay. From beginning to end, the trail, most of which is paved and wheelchair-accessible, runs about six kilometres. The manicured grounds and winding ways offer a constant stream of things to see on the water and in the air, be they natural or of human origin.

Biking or hiking the trail never ceases to entertain, as there is always something different going on. Catching the Harbour Ferry, either for transport or as a harbour cruise, is an experience in and of itself, carrying the visitor into the heart of historic Victoria. Check out the special offerings, including the Pickle Pub Crawl.

The Trek bike shop (trekbikesvictoria.com, 250-380-7877) is next door to the guesthouse and offers both bike repairs and rentals. A 24-hour rental costs $75.

ESTABLISHMENT 18

The Gorge Pointe Pub

1075 Tillicum Road, Victoria

Webpage –
Services –

1-250-386-5500
gorgepointepub.com
wi-fi, wheelchair-accessible with
wheelchair-accessible washrooms
and handicapped parking

Location
South side of the Gorge, just across the Tillicum Narrows Bridge. Ample
parking is available on site.

What makes Gorge Pointe Pub unique: location, theme, décor and
family-friendly
Located central to walkways and parks along Victoria's Gorge Waterway, a long finger of the sea with a rich history and singular appeal,
the Gorge Pointe Pub is an ideal gathering spot for those seeking a day
along or in the water.

There has been a hotel or pub of some sort at this site for over a century, surviving Prohibition and reinventing itself in the 1950s, when owners named Mauer, Maggiora and Politano returned the building to use
as a popular beer parlour. A 1952 photo shows a resplendent, substantial hotel bounded by forest. In 1993, the present-day Gorge Pointe
Pub arose on the site to begin its own story. The Mediterranean-style
structure, with many windows, is but a stone's throw from the Gorge, with its parks, walkways and scenic and historic features.

The doors open to an interior lined in deep red woods, with ample seating options for groups large to small. Booth, table and bar seating is divided between two larger rooms, coupled with a raised dais section and the "Lounge," comfortably furnished in retro style. A large, seasonal patio that would easily be at home in the Mediterranean beckons at the rear. A two-sided fireplace in rich woods captures the eye as you enter, and light pours in from a bank of windows. The place exudes a sense of comfort for all seasons.

Historic photos of the Gorge and the old hotel line the entrance wall, and a unique set of climbing photos adorns the small pool room. Quite by chance, several of the pub's owners happened to be mountaineers, and photos from their international adventures give substance to their achievements.

Gorge Pointe Pub prides itself on supporting the vibrant Victoria and area craft beer industry, sporting products from the Phillips, Vancouver Island, Driftwood, Lighthouse, Hoyne, and Category 12 breweries, plus the internationally popular Guinness.

In a tilt to changing times, minors are allowed within the premises until 4 p.m. Today the pub draws customers from the many folk who live in the area as well as visitors who come, like so many before them, to enjoy the features of the Gorge near the hotel's front door.

Earning your beer

The Gorge is beautiful and enigmatic, whether it's experienced from land or water. It has drawn people for thousands of years.

The Songhees people used the gorge to sustain life and spirit, as proven by a midden found in the area that dates back 4,100 years. Legend tells of a young girl, Camossung (Camosun) who was turned to rock by the spirit Haylas and left to guard the Gorge. After years uncounted, the prominent rock explained by the legend was blasted away in the 1960s by a local non-aboriginal to facilitate water traffic. Until that time the reversing falls, which still pass swiftly through Tillicum Narrows at 17 kilometres per hour during the tide change, were even faster and steeper.

The Gorge continues to play host to the Head of the Gorge Regatta in October, and Victoria Harbour Ferries run a Gorge excursion trip. Historically, it was even more alive with regattas, dare-devil diving, water tours to the Japanese Tea Gardens and boating, as photos on display at the pub attest. The care and attention the waterway is getting today suggests it will continue to attract new visitors as more people learn of its redevelopment.

Esquimalt Gorge Park includes walkways, playgrounds, and a stunning Japanese Garden. Across the water, the Kinsmen Gorge Park offers hiking and viewpoints. Hikers can burn off kilometres trekking the long Gorge Waterway trail and find their way back, via a loop through the residential section, to bring them full around to the bridge and pub. Historical plaques, sculptures, tended gardens, beaches, boat put-ins and the busy waterway keep the eyes occupied while the feet go about their business. Tuft-headed mergansers, bobble-headed buffleheads, sleek cormorants and nagging gulls entertained us on our walk. Hikers, bikers, photographers, birders, kayakers, canoeists... there's something for everyone.

And if you like those parklands with holes in them, there is Gorge Vale Golf Club (gorgevalegolf.com) within walking distance of the pub.

ESTABLISHMENT 19

Four Mile House Brew Pub

199 Island Highway, Victoria

	1-250-479-2514
Webpage —	fourmilehouse.com
Services —	wi-fi, wheelchair-accessible with wheel chair-accessible washrooms

Location
On the Island Highway at View Royal Avenue; left turns are facilitated by traffic lights. Offers ample parking and good bus service (Admirals Road #14).

What makes Four Mile House Pub unique: location, history, theme, architecture, hauntings (?), and it's a brew pub

If rumours be true, Elizabeth Montgomery still inhabits the dwelling she saw rise from the earth 150 years ago, when she and husband Peter Calvert first built upon the hill overlooking the portage route between the sea and Victoria's inland Gorge. And she is apparently not alone; Four Mile has been rated one of the top 10 haunted buildings in B.C.

The fourth-oldest standing building in Victoria, the Four Mile was constructed as a way station along the Sooke Road, set on the crest of steep Four Mile Hill to make it convenient for thirsty travellers struggling up the incline. One story has it that the station had a parrot who hollered "Whoa" at approaching horses, who instinctively turned in for welcome roadhouse fare.

Inside, above the pub's brick fireplace, framed in arched brick, the stained-

glass image of the sad "White Lady" now surveys a changed world. Hers is the story of a captain's wife, a relative of the Calverts staying at the inn, who in failing health eagerly searched the horizon every day at Thetis Point, awaiting her husband's return. Her ghost is said to still be watching from the "White Lady" rocks for the one who returned too late to shore.

Other spirits include the phantom customer who leaves his chair slightly askew after his visits and pioneer Jake Matteson, said to be the original stakeholder of the property in the 1840s. He died suddenly, and legend has it he left behind a stash of gold hidden in a well. Though wells have been found, no gold has appeared. To these eerie tales are added the sounds of footsteps, tapping teaspoons and items disappearing, reappearing, and being moved about.

There has been seen, in broad daylight, the figure of a woman in a full-length gown staring out over the garden from an upstairs window. The belief is that she is Peter's daughter, Margaret.
Above all of these is the essence of Margaret's mother, Elizabeth, a healer whose touch colours the mood of Four Mile. In the early days, Elizabeth took to learning from the wisdom of the local Songhees First Nation, mastering their language and healing lore. So strong was her influence that when she died the indigenous people attended her funeral in numbers and conducted a Mask Dance in her honour, a tribute seldom offered to settler people. Her healing aura is said to pervade the building.

The Inn prospered until World War I and Prohibition. In the 1940s it earned its way as the Green Lantern (the "Coziest Cabaret in Town"), with a brothel operating upstairs. Police raids put an end to the operation and the house languished until 1979, when present-day owners Wendy and Graham Haymes took over and gave the spirits more welcoming accommodation. In 1988, it opened as a pub, and to this has been added a restaurant, downstairs sports bar, liquor outlet and, as of 2014, a brew pub.

The Tudor-style exterior gives way inside to a broad English pub theme, housing the few and the many in comfy niches and a grander, barrel-vaulted great room. Here an opulent chandelier sparkles above and heavy wood wainscotting joins period wallpaper and open-beam construction to create an atmosphere of well-tended hominess. Antiques, stained glass, memorabilia and posters adorn the walls and bar, including two old licence plates from 1913 and 1914, which were owned by the Calverts. Side rooms allow the Four Mile to accommodate patrons in numbers without feeling crowded. Complementing all is the all-season, enclosed wrap-round deck, allowing for quieter retreat.

The Four Mile joins an ever-expanding family of Victoria craft breweries and now turns 17 of its 18 taps to its own products, all brewed to high standards and free of preservatives and additives. Every second Friday night is cask night, which sees a "firkin" of non-carbonated beer opened for attending patrons—a unique flavour experience.
All this in an atmosphere where spirits of many types are fairly brewed and kindly directed.

<u>Earning your beer</u>
Beside the pub is a trail leading into Portage Park and down to the peaceful beach, long a place of habitation for local First Nations people. From these shores the White Lady stood and gazed forlornly out to sea. On our foggy-day visit, a lone kingfisher huddled on a thin branch watching the calm waters and a silent blue heron gliding past. Close your eyes here and be transported back. The trail leads on to connect with the E&N side trail, which already attracts hikers and bikers and will do so even more when opened from Langford to downtown Victoria. It leads right by the Four Mile.
The only thing missing is a parrot to say "Whoa."

ESTABLISHMENT 20

The Six Mile Pub

494 Old Island Highway, Victoria
                       1-250-478-3121
Webpage –   sixmilepub.com
Services –   wi-fi, wheelchair-accessible with wheel
                       chair-accessible washrooms

Location
Old Island Highway heading toward Sooke at Six Mile Road intersection (lights). There is ample parking and good late-running bus service.

What makes the Six Mile Pub unique: history, location, hauntings, theme, decor, river setting and a menu using sustainable ingredients from local producers (including herbs and vegetables from their own garden and honey from their own apiary). Kitchen is microwave-free.

The road is a bit busier here than in 1855, when Bill Parsons purchased the old Hudson's Bay Company property (40 acres) for 39 pounds sterling. It later spanned Millstream Creek, gaining its first bridge in 1863. Having garnered a liquor licence in 1856, the Parson's Bridge Hotel takes the honours as B.C.'s oldest pub. It would have many owners during its colourful history before the present one took over in 2002, and he now holds the record as the longest serving publican in Six Miles' history.

One of its most colourful proprietors was Jim Price, who ran it during the days of Prohibition and managed to host secret meetings and a little bootlegging to keep lips moist and dollars flowing. It has seen fires and renovations and remained the local constant while the community surrounding it grew. Its Tudor carriage-house style—half-timbered,

(photo courtesy Six Mile Pub)

with a shake roof and an old English red phone box near the entrance—gives away its British theme.

Open the doors and the theme continues inside, with dark woods, brick-framed gas fireplaces, board and stucco walls, adorned with prints and photos of the Isles and local history. The dark wood bar, awash with a sea of brew taps and topped by stained-glass panels, is guarded by somber-faced figureheads looking aloof. There's a wealth of space, deceptively divided into sections by hearths, raised daises and corners. A riverside patio and separate games room afford even more space and options, while bar, bench and table seating provides ample choice for any group size. Set apart from the more boisterous adult conversation is a family-friendly eatery housing up to 80 patrons.

On the walls hang historic photos of the building in its many forms over the years, previous owners (including Parsons), and reflections of earlier times. The wrought-iron spiral staircase seems almost youthful, though it has been in place for 70 to 80 years. Perhaps most stunning is the copy of the original deed ceding Hudson's Bay land to William Parsons, dated 1855.

Twenty-two beer taps show a strong bent toward local craft-brewing businesses, with Phillips, Driftwood, Lighthouse, Hoyne (all Victoria breweries) and Tofino breweries taking up eight. Toss in Guinness on tap as well. The operation takes pride in its food service, to the point of maintaining a small organic garden on the property and its own beehives—a certain connection to the operations of roadhouses past.

Popular in the neighbourhood, the Six Mile also has a following among cyclists, hikers, kayakers and canoeists who follow the Galloping Goose Trail or Millstream Creek to reach the pub. Bike racks, with complimentary locks offered by the pub, and a spot for boaters to pull their craft ashore reflect the pub's accommodating attitude.

And perhaps there are others who still inhabit these familiar environs. There have been rumours of ghosts about the place—not surprising, given its age and the adventures it has seen. Both customers and staff have claimed to witness appari-

tions either seen or eerily sensed. Antique items have been mysteriously moved about in a locked display cabinet.

Perhaps from an upper-floor window it is the memory of a vastly different time that watches a modern world whizzing by over the concrete bridge. For more than 150 years, people have come and gone here—and perhaps not all have gone.

<u>Earning your beer</u>
The Galloping Goose Trail, an incredible passage running from Swartz Bay to Sooke River and beyond, is minutes away on foot, as is Thetis Lake Park. It is a compelling draw for hikers and cyclists, groups of whom enjoy pleasurable exercise punctuated with a good meal and beverage at the Six Mile. Add to this, Millstream Creek, which runs below the pub and passes on to the ocean beyond.

ESTABLISHMENT **21**

The 17 Mile Pub

5126 Sooke Road, Victoria
1-250-642-5942
Webpage – 17milehouse.com
Services – wi-fi, wheelchair-accessibility with wheelchair-accessible washrooms

<u>Location</u>
Seven kilometres from the Sooke River Bridge heading east; 13 kilometres from the lights at Sooke Road and Veterans Memorial Way heading west. There is parking on both sides of the road. City bus #61 provides a regular transport option.

<u>What makes the 17 Mile Pub unique:</u> history, hauntings (?), setting, location and its own special theme

There are places where character and uniqueness ooze like cool sand between the toes on a West Coast beach. Such a place is the 17 Mile Pub, a spot cloaked in mystery and atmosphere.

Its solitary setting, wrapped about by forest and steep hills, catches the eye as it rounds into view. Its worn but tended entrance is adorned with two plaques speaking to its history. This has been an authentic roadhouse in the truest of English tradition since it first rose along the wagon road to Sooke and the gold fields of Leechtown, back in 1894, whence came its current name.

It went by different names when it was first opened by Edward Cutler, joining four other local roadhouses (including the 4 Mile and 6 Mile) blessed with Royal

Charters. It has been called the British Ensign and the Royal Ensign, and has witnessed not just the drawing of taps, but also lessons and lectures as a school and a home for religious teaching.

Above the entrance steps the welcoming red door is embedded with a poured glass of Guinness rendered in stained glass, adorned with a proud "17." Within are more stained-glass creations locally made and incorporated in the renovations carried out by the present owners. The themed interior décor is perhaps best described as West Coast 17 Mile, leaving the sense that many a passing era has left its mark on the building. Well-worn wood floors give way to a colourful, '50s-era tiled section; above the dark-hued wainscotting, timeless wallpaper and memorabilia contend for attention with historic photos.

A windowed seating area overlooking the garden and patio features paintings and prints of the old pub. Beer steins hang above, old bottles line shelves, and a small room, once part of the original residence, retains a homey feeling enhanced by a wood-burning fireplace. It's said that the ghost of one of the two matrons of the pub has been seen watching the road, as if waiting for travellers. Another, friendly, ghost is said to be the boyfriend of former owner Mary Jackson, who ran the pub from 1910 until her death on June 20, 1941. Allegedly he either hanged himself in the building or killed himself outside on the hill.

The family connection to the 17 Mile runs deep, and on display are two photos of long-serving matrons of the pub. Mrs. Mary E. Jackson was followed by Edith Mary "Ma" Wilson, who oversaw the operation from 1941 until her death in February 1970. It is said she passed away in her rocking chair in the main-floor sitting room. Her family retains ownership of the building, and grandsons Jeremy and Justin Wilson are part of the present pub ownership group. Their mother, Noni Wilson, who has since passed, ran the pub from 1971 to 2005.

It was Ma Wilson who installed the unique tile flooring, which once carried the weight of a grand piano. Bullet holes, since covered up, in the fireplace room attest to the heady early days of the pub. Check out accounts of the pub's history on its webpage.

Stories of Ma's assertiveness are the stuff of legend. It is said she kept a loaded shotgun nearby and was firm with local patrons—allowing them only one or two drinks and then sending them home, unless they were drivers, and then they got only one drink. A feature collection book of articles and items on the pub was kept at the bar for viewing for many a year until one classless individual stole it. The owners plan on putting together a new one—worth reading for the hauntings alone.

Today's pub bears vestiges of that history but keeps a hand in the present. The place exudes a sense of fun. Though seemingly not large, it accommodates many in its four clearly defined sections, plus a pool and darts room and the outside lawn/patio area, which invites patrons to play volleyball, horseshoes, bocce ball and or a game on the outdoor pool table. Every July, the pub hosts the annual Sookapalooza, which provides ongoing outdoor entertainment.

Inside seating, including at the double-sided bar, provides space for larger and smaller groups, with the separate, homey fireplace room lending a sense of warm privacy, the essence of a personal parlour. Island beer on tap includes brews from Victoria breweries Phillips and Lighthouse, a rotating IPA tap, plus famed Guinness. Live entertainment occurs every Friday night.

If there are ghosts in these walls, I suspect they enjoy the buoyant atmosphere, even as they find rest in its secluded setting when all the living folk have gone home. Time just adds to the atmosphere.

Earning your beer

Within a short distance of the pub stretches the Galloping Goose Trail and options for cyclists and hikers, plus the Adrena Zip Line adventure centre (adrenalinezip.com). The offerings of East Sooke Park are nearby (east sookepark.com)

ESTABLISHMENT 22

Port Renfrew Pub

17310 Parkinson Road, Port Renfrew

1-844-647-5541

Webpage –   wildrenfrew.com

Services –   wi-fi, wheelchair-accessible with wheelchair-accessible washrooms

Location

Take Highway 14 out of Sooke to the fork in the road at Port San Juan. Right takes you to the parking lot for the resort and pub, and left takes you to Botanical Beach. Two hours from Victoria.

What makes Port Renfrew Pub unique: view, setting, location, history
The cedar board-and-batten façade of the Port Renfrew pub and restaurant rise above the long finger of the resort wharf pointing into the heart of Port San Juan. The first hotel arose by the wharf in the heady mining days of the 1890s, but 1920 saw it perish in flames, to be replaced in 1927. Its rough-and-tumble existence, which included at least one fatal patron confrontation, was pushed into the 21st century when the old ramshackle structure was replaced in 2006 with a new building offering pub and restaurant service. The hotel rooms are gone, replaced by cabins closer to the waters.

Seaborne traffic remained the norm until 1954, when the road from Victoria finally reached the small community. Even now, it has an air of relaxing isolation from the hectic outside world.

(photo courtesy Port Renfrew Pub)

Tall and weather-polished, the exterior belies the contemporary decor and design of the interior. High ceilings with open beams loom over wainscotted walls and rich cedar finishings. Skylights bathe the spacious interior in natural light, complementing the effect of the large-framed windows. Table and chair plus bar seating accommodates many a patron, with more seating on the outer deck, which faces over a stream that empties into the bay. The bright, contemporary bar is a length of rich cedar guarded by a singularly impressive piece of First Nations art, the work of Sooke artist Gordie Planes. The large totem pole outside is the work of local artist Bill Khunley Sr. A separate, grand niche with a maritime theme accommodates a pool table and dartboards.

More First Nations artwork adorns the walls, and the long corridor leading to the restaurant is lined with photos and name plates honouring some of the many ships that fell victim to the wild West Coast shore off Pachena Point, famed as the Graveyard of the Pacific. The Soquel, with loss of captain and wife in 1909; the HMS Condor, with all 100 hands; and the passenger ship Valencia in 1906, with all 117 passengers and crew, were among the many reasons for installing a lighthouse here, and the foundation of the famed West Coast Trail. Other photos include shots of early Port Renfrew, with visiting steamships drawn aside the long wharf, and previous hotels.

Vancouver Island craft beers on tap are represented by Vancouver Island and Salt Spring Island breweries, usually complemented by Guinness. On special nights, live music enlivens the atmosphere.
Fishing derbies occupy the summer months up to October, when the Coho derby signals the season's end. Big cash prizes draw attention, and part of the proceeds go to the nearby fish hatchery. Here, too, the local crabbing is acclaimed.

It should be noted that Port Renfrew received its name in 1895 when the title of Lord Renfrew, who had intended to settle crofters here, replaced that of San Juan. Sitting on the outside deck, drinking in the close-to-wilderness setting, you can feel far from the madding world. And should you wish to use the restaurant deck, the

(photo courtesy Port Renfrew Pub)

expanse of Port San Juan and the Island mountains behind are there to impress.

Earning your beer
This is spectacular country for fishermen, hikers, kayakers, photographers, naturalists, birders and their ilk. So strong is the draw, tourism has overtaken fishing and logging as the economic mainstay.

Nearby is the western terminus of the Juan de Fuca Trail, built in the 1990s and open to everything form trekking the length to short day trips. Its more famed northern kin is the West Coast Trail, created in 1907 to assist in rescuing those shipwrecked along these dangerous shores—a trail so popular and demanding that trekkers must apply and register to take on the arduous trek. (env.bc.ca/bcparks/explore/parkpgs/juan_de_fuca)

The Ancient Forest Alliance has preserved, close by, an area known as Avatar Grove, which houses the Red Creek Fir (the world's tallest Douglas fir) and the San Juan Spruce, Canada's largest Sitka spruce. (ancientrainforestguide.com/big-trees.php?ID=1)

A short distance from the pub is Botanical Beach Provincial Park, where low tide reveals a a mass of sculpted rock and little mini-aquariums holding a colourful array of sea life.

Surfers take to the waters at Sombrio Beach and Jordan River to the south. Campers favour sites on Fairy Lake, Lizard Lake and at the Pacheedhat Campground, which is visible across the water from the pub, particularly in the evening, when the campfire glow crosses the bay. Paddle sports and whale-watching options are offered off the dock near the Seaside Cottages gift shop.

Many people are now incorporating a visit to the pub with the paved circle tour, which allows drivers to go from Victoria via Port Renfrew through Lake Cowichan to Duncan and back to Victoria.

For more, check the site portrenfrew.com.

ESTABLISHMENT 23

Axe & Barrel Brewing Company

2323 Millstream Road, (Langford) Victoria
1-250-474-1989
Webpage – axeandbarrel.com
Services – wi-fi, wheelchair-accessible with wheel chair-accessible washrooms

Location
Just east off the Trans Canada Highway, on Millstream Road. Can't miss the distinctive log structure.

What makes the Axe and Barrel unique: architecture, decor, grounds, and its own craft beer

Since 1989, this eye-catching work of art, set amid well-tended grounds, has blended wood, stone and greenery into a singular union that would stand out in any setting. It would not suffer in the company of, say, the Emerald Lake Lodge or the Prince of Wales Hotel at Waterton Lakes National Park. This ageless edifice was built under the watchful eye of master craftsman Pat Lintaman. As with the stone grandeur of Rattenbury creations, it's pleasing to see how well its creative construction has been preserved with care over many years.

Expenses were not spared in the original building, which features wool carpeting and fixtures and fittings of solid brass. Sustainability and local resourcing were fundamental parts of the design and construction, long before those became the mantra for environmental responsibility. The Douglas fir logs were from 60-year-old second growth, logged 44 miles away in Cowichan, and the cedar siding, roof, trim, and window and

door frames were all provided from the builder's own sustainably managed woodlot. The Axe & Barrel will still be proudly standing by the time new growth has replaced the materials used to build it.

After a flux and flow in ownership, the Loghouse, as it was then known, came into the sole ownership of realtor Ron Cheeke in 2007. He has continued the history of fine care of the building and grounds, having renovated and reopened it as the Axe and Barrel Brewing Company in 2016. The grand structure has been enhanced with a 1,300-square-foot patio seating 60 patrons, fanned by leafy palm trees, with the season extended by outdoor heaters. The adjacent liquor store, known as "Liquor Planet," boasts 14,000 square feet. The latest addition is the pub's own craft brewery, the Axe & Barrel Brewing Company, producing eight labels: Langford Lager, Speedway RPA, Tessier's Witbier, award-winning King Kolsch, Hopline Bling, Westshore IPA, Fruity Mother Pucker and Knockers Porter. This adds to the other craft beers represented on tap, which currently include products of Lighthouse, Vancouver Island, and Phillips breweries, all of Victoria.

Inside, this world of polished wood and rich finishings induces a sense of laid-back party time without the accompanying hangover. Every part of it speaks of solidness and durability. Niches and larger rooms accommodate groups big and small with table, bench and bar seating enough for 217 patrons. The TVs are tuned to sports stations, but this is more than a sports bar; the size and decor are equally inviting to those seeking a quieter brew or meal. The palm tree-edged patio with outdoor heaters enhances the options and appeal.

Entertainment includes a regular Friday-night rock'n'roll band getting folks up and dancing, a Tuesday-night open mike, plus a host of evening activities including music bingo on Saturdays. If the appeal of locally brewed craft beer were not enough, the beauty of this edifice set within tended grounds alone makes it worth a visit.

Earning your beer
Within easy hiking and biking distance is Millstream Creek Trail, and dedicated bike lanes connect you to Bear Mountain Parkway and the golf course beyond. A host of lakes and parks are nearby, including Florence, Langford and Thetis Lakes—all within hiking and cycling distance. For details and maps, check crd.bc.ca.

SECTION TWO Mid-Island South

ESTABLISHMENT 24

The Cobblestone Inn

3566 Holland Ave. Cobble Hill

                      1-250-743-4232

Webpage –   cobblestone.ca

Services –   wi-fi, wheelchair-accessible with wheel chair-accessible washrooms

Location

In Cobble Hill Village, off of Cobble Hill Road and across from the village cenotaph.

What makes the Cobblestone unique: setting, theme, history, location, family-friendly, and permanent patrons

There are places so popular some patrons simply refuse to go home. Given that the Cobblestone has been in the same family for over 30 years and that the location was a village centre long before that, when a local creamery occupied the site, you can appreciate the sense of place it exudes.

The creamery began operations in the 1890s and lasted until the 1940s, while the pub came to life in 1983 and has been in the same family hands ever since. Original builder John Ross "Bud" Lee still looks on from his print perched atop the brick fireplace, and on occasion visits to oversee his creation.

The sizeable pub includes a grand common room to accommodate dancing and larger groups, while also granting patrons more intimate space. A British theme with Tudor-style beam and stucco is complemented by

an eclectic assortment of features, including a massive buffalo head looming over one fireplace. Historic and theme-oriented photos and prints (fishing, logging) adorn the walls, along with horse brasses and etched glass. Activities include pool and darts.

Friday and Saturday entertainment includes music and comedy.
The pub takes pains to create a comfortable environment for the varying groups frequenting it at various times of the day and week. Very much a village social centre, it also attracts groups from the region, such as golfers from Arbutus Ridge, senior hiking groups, Remembrance Day crowds after the nearby cenotaph service, and attendees from the Cobble Hill Fair, which has been running for more than a century. Safety and convenience are enhanced by a shuttle bus service provided Fridays and Saturdays. The pub is child-friendly until 3 p.m. and began opening at 9 a.m. for breakfast in the fall of 2017.

Island craft beers are represented by Phillips and Hoyne breweries out of Victoria, Red Arrow out of Duncan and Cowichan Valley's own Merridale Cider on tap.

As this has been such a comfortable community centre over many years, you can see why two former patrons decided to set up permanent residence here. The ashes of the two now call the Cobblestone Inn home. One person's final abode is a Lucky Lager can, while his compatriot decided to remain sauced in an HP Sauce bottle. Could prove an interesting trend.

Earning your beer
The village is close to the waters and beaches of Shawnigan Lake, but even closer are the hiking, biking and horse trails of Cobble Hill Park. The 2.5-kilometre climb to Cobble Hill provides for a panoramic viewpoint at the summit (331 metres, or 1,086 feet) with the opportunity to put in many more miles by exploring the web of trails amid the trees. The park offers parking, washroom facilities, a doggie park and a small mountain bike course at the base.

The village, park and pub have much to look forward to if and when the Esquimalt and Nanaimo Railway resumes service linking Victoria to Courtenay. An easy and pleasurable day riding up from Victoria or down from Courtenay would reignite the day-tripper crowds that historically enjoyed weekend train excursions.

ESTABLISHMENT 25

Cowichan Bay Pub

1695 Cowichan Bay Road, Cowichan Bay
                              1-250-748-2330
Webpage –   baypub.ca
Services –   wi-fi, wheelchair-accessible with wheel
                              chair-accessible washrooms

<u>Location</u>
At the south end of town, on Cowichan Bay Road, overlooking the harbour. Bike racks and underground parking

<u>What makes the Cowichan Bay Pub unique:</u> view, location, setting and Cowichan Bay

Its tended modernity belies the fact the Cowichan Bay Pub has owned its spectacular view of bay and mountain for 40 years plus, though it has gone by a plethora of names, including the Black Douglas and Windjammer. Its bank of expansive windows allows a flood of natural light to complement the view of looming Mount Tzouhalem, with its tall white cross—a Catholic stations-of-the-cross legacy of present-day Providence Farm—distant, blunt-faced Mount Prevost, and the busy harbour. Great blue herons stalk Fisherman's Wharf, seals pop up curious heads, occasional pods of orcas cruise the bay and, in season, great sea lions barkingly assert their presence. It is an unhindered view as alive as it is dramatic—and all the more so outside on the deck.

The tended, contemporary interior offers table, upholstered booth, and bar seating, sectioned off around the central bar to allow a greater degree of privacy for those who wish it. Two pool tables and dartboards have their own niche, while a gas fireplace warms the other side of the bar. A wood dance floor lies ready for use when live music prods patrons to let loose.

There is live jazz every Thursday, live background music on Friday, and featured bands on various occasions. Island pride is reflected in the taps turned to three Victoria-produced craft beers: two taps for Phillips and one each to Driftwood and Hoyne breweries. Revealing the growing popularity of craft beers, Phillips and Driftwood go number one and number two, respectively, in demand. Prawns drawn from the waters outside the window have a place of honour in a menu that stresses the use of local products and suppliers, reflecting the great pride taken in the pub's cuisine. The Cow Bay Pub offers a seaside welcome in a setting where you can sit back and enjoy the entertainment of the bay and/or sun-setting splendour in contemporary comfort.

Earning Your Beer

Including the Cow Bay Pub in a trip to the seaside town of Cowichan Bay is part of a total experience. It is a town on the water like no other in the area. Homes and buildings jut out into the bay on tide-washed pylons, and the long string of boats hugging the shoreline leaves no doubt this is a working town of the waters. Art galleries, restaurants, whale-watching tours, coffee shops, bakeries, fishmongers, curio shops, kayak rentals and more are strung along the narrow band of road. A maritime museum stretches upon its long pier, pushing its nose long into the bay. Here you can take in detailed scale-model reproductions of sailing and working ships back to the classic days of sail.

At the north end of town is the Cowichan Estuary Nature Centre and bird-watching station. In the summer months, consider an excursion by sea to tranquil Genoa Bay via Greylag Boat Shuttle Tours. One mark of its uniqueness is that Cowichan Bay in 2009 became the first community in North America to join Cittaslow, an international organization of 187 towns in 28 countries that have committed to taking the time to celebrate community history and traditions, embrace craftsmanship and environmental responsibility, and encourage a high quality of life. For more information on Cowichan Bay, check cowichanbay.com.

ESTABLISHMENT 26

Lion Rampant Scottish Pub

6777 Beaumont Avenue, Maple Bay
1-250-746-5422
Webpage — lionrampant.ca
Services — wi-fi, wheelchair-accessible with wheelchair-accessible washrooms

Location
On the waterfront at Maple Bay, past the government dock and beside the little community park. Float-plane service to Vancouver and Vancouver International Airport is provided by Salt Spring Air and Harbour Air, which also serve Victoria and Nanaimo.

What makes the Lion Rampant unique: view, location, Scotch selection, setting and Scottish theme

We are used to impressive scenery here on the Islands, so it takes a bit to make the eyes open wider. The view from the windows and outdoor patio of the Lion Rampant at Maple Bay does that; it's like gazing o'er a Scottish loch. Across Sansum Narrows rises Mount Baynes, at 1,930 feet (588 metres) the highest peak on Salt Spring Island. Better known locally as Mount Maxwell, its steep face looms majestically over land and water. Sheltered Maple Bay presents a more pastoral scene, with its wide arms embracing the tiny community and its marinas.

The Lion Rampant rises above the bay and its own private dock, welcom-

ing boaters large and small. Beside it, the small, shaded, grassy community park offers summer sun, swimming and picnicking in this postcard setting. Though it appears unassuming from the outside, when you step into the pub you are immediately struck by its spaciousness, by the rectangular bar with a marble counter resplendent under a bright tin-plate ceiling, and by the stunning view. Reigning at the bar sits Jevon, the rampant lion statue and mascot. Counterpart statue Sir Bryan rules the outer empire.

The new owners took over the historic Brigantine Pub the end of March 2014 and reopened after extensive renovations on May 9, 2014. The Scottish theme is highlighted by wall prints of a lion rampant, Scotch thistle, Scottish-themed menu items (oh, Ode to a Haggis!), Guinness & Gunn Scotch Ale on tap, and an elixir-of-the-gods offering of high-end Scotch. One of only four bottles of 35-year-old-plus Port Allen Scotch available in B.C. holds court here, with a tasty dram's worth setting the imbiber back $295 plus tax. The famed distillery of the Isle of Islay closed its doors in 1984, so there's none more to be had, laddie.

The 14 taps offer the craft beers of Vancouver Island breweries Driftwood, Vancouver Island, Phillips, Lighthouse, Hoyne, and Moon Under Water from Victoria, plus Salt Spring Island Brewery and Longwood from Nanaimo. Topping it off are taps for Cowichan Valley's own Merridale Cider and Guinness. Add to this an incredible array of 40 brands of Scotch.

The pub is roomy, with broad windows facing the bay and its famed view. It offers a wide array of seating convenient for groups, individuals or couples, amid a casual, wood-accented setting. The expansive outer deck facing the waters is comfortably appointed with tables and chairs and a comfy couch, leaving one to drink in the view and enjoy the breeze in sheltered ease.

The Brig's Celtic-enhanced festivities include annual St. Patrick's Day and Robbie Burns Day celebrations. Live entertainment on the weekends features a Celtic folk music theme. In a nod to this new age of responsible imbibing, the Lion Rampant offers a shuttle service every Friday and Saturday night.

This setting and its wonderful view has been around for a long time and earned a reputation sufficient to bring in groups from afar, including car clubs from Victoria, kayakers, and boaters, as well as many a local. It is easy to see why car clubbers would like the place, as

you can get here on pastoral, winding back roads that are scenic in their own right. If you can't find yourself lounging by a true loch with a beer in hand, the Lion Rampant can transport you there in atmosphere.

Earning Your Beer

Walking distance from the pub are kayak and Hobie craft rentals at Wilderness Kayaking (wilderness-kayaking.com), which also offers guided tours. A government wharf provides further tie-ups for visitors, whatever their craft, and a walkable pebble beach spreads from the Lion Rampant to the government wharf. For the ambitious there is a hiking trail running all the way from Crofton to Maple Bay, which can be done in whole or in part, offering stunning views over the Narrows to Salt Spring. For a shorter trek to a stunning viewpoint, the trail can be picked up at the end of Arbutus Avenue, a healthy walk from the pub. Maple Mountain crests at 1,657 feet (505 metres).

ESTABLISHMENT 27

Shipyard Restaurant & Pub

#18 – 6145 Genoa Bay Road, Duncan
1-250-746-1026
Webpage – shipyardrestaurant.com
Services – wi-fi, wheelchair-accessible with wheelchair-accessible washrooms

Location

At the Maple Bay Marina on Genoa Bay Road. Harbour Air provides float plane air service from Maple Bay to Vancouver, Vancouver International Airport, Victoria and Nanaimo, while Salt Spring Air connects to Vancouver downtown and Vancouver International Airport.

What makes the Shipyard unique: setting, location, architecture

There are unique pubs located at marinas. The Shipyard goes a step further, in being thoroughly of the marina it calls home. A pub in form and function that speaks of the sea and boats and does so with a cozy comfort welcoming even to landlubbers. It rests easily amid the workings of a busy marina built of the same bones.

Laurie Sellwood has run the Shipyard for the past 14 years, managing both the pub and the upper-floor restaurant, whose many windows gaze out upon a sea of masts and a village of floating homes. Creatively housed in a converted boat hangar, the Shipyard is adorned inside and out with reminders of a watery world. Life rings, retired engines, rope-wrapped posts, propellers and tool chests dot the simple exterior and give way to an eclectic hodgepodge of sea regalia once you pass the threshold into the welcoming hold of the nautical inner sanctum. Models, paintings, and photos

of ships of sail and motor line the walls and shelves, along with ship's bells, plaques, globes, maps, a large helm and more. The well-worn wood floor retains vestiges of a world map painted on its heavily trodden slats, and the open-beam ceiling reveals its history as a workaday building reborn in a more leisurely incarnation. The floor, ceiling and wood-slat walls all converge on "the Bridge"—the inviting bar and colourful centre of activity, where regular patrons gather to sit or stand. Spread throughout the remainder of the pub are tables and chairs and high chair seating centred on raised shelving wrapped around posts. Though small, the Shipyard makes good use of its space, finding room for an electric fireplace, TV, and, on Friday nights, live entertainment.

In season, the glass-enclosed patio shelters patrons from wind while giving full access to the smell of the sea and the sights and sounds of one of the largest marinas in B.C. Flags from distant locations have long graced the piers of this well-known island, where visitors savour the peacefulness of its sheltered waters and emerald-clad hills. In season and out, the Friday entertainment here, with no cover charge, has become a pub staple with both marina folk and local islanders, who come early to get a seat in the close quarters. Jazz, blues, rock, bluegrass and other genres bring out their unique fans, as do the regular performers their faithful following. Check out the webpage to discover the scheduled acts. Sound knows few confines, so the upper-floor restaurant patrons are equally entertained. To add to the island charm, Island craft beer by Phillips and Hoyne of Victoria, Red Arrow of Duncan and Merridale Cider are on tap, comprising half of the eight taps.

Ample parking makes for ease of access. Informal, unassuming and cozy, the Shipyard exudes a quiet appeal that makes coming back an easy choice.

Earning your beer
Just getting to the pub makes for a pleasurable drive through pastoral and wilderness settings threaded along the coast before landing you alongside the bay, facing the rising face of Salt Spring Island. Kayak and Hobie craft rentals are available (wilderness-kayaking.com); diving, fishing and hiking the trails of Maple Mountain and its scenic viewpoints can work up a thirst and hunger. Come in May and you get to see the annual wooden boat festival (maplebaymarina.com/events). Exploring the marina itself—its boats, float homes and idyllic setting looking out upon the pastoral bay beyond little Chisholm Island—offers much to boat lovers, photographers, and anyone with an appreciation of beauty.

ESTABLISHMENT **28**

Craig Street Brew Pub

25 Craig Street, Duncan

	1-250-737-2337
Webpage –	craigstreet.ca
Services –	wi-fi, wheelchair-accessible with wheel chair-accessible washrooms

Location
Located near Government Street and Craig Street in old Duncan.

What makes the Craig Street Brew Pub unique: architecture, history and Duncan's only brew pub.

Walking into the Craig Street Brew Pub is rather like walking into Dr. Who's Tardis: it feels like a entering a time warp and and seems a lot bigger on the inside than it appears outside. Carved out of an old clothing store dating back to the 1940s, this contemporary pub incorporates vestiges of its lineage inside, offering a bow to an even more distant past with its 100-year-old bar. This is all in harmony with a modern design that accommodates a good number of patrons, yet affords more intimate space for those seeking it.

Three indoor floor levels are complemented by an outside rooftop patio and street-level patio. The top floor, replete with a bar and its own washrooms, is ideal for social or professional gatherings. There is even a small bookstore/library feature centred near a big-screen TV, with a strong hockey bias. Gathered along the mezzanine walls are historical photos recalling the time when the building served as a livery stable, gradually evolving into a gas station and other incarnations, including Pow-

(photo courtesy Craig St Brew Pub)

ell's Men's Wear, before arriving as a pub. That it stands on revitalized Craig Street in Duncan's old town only adds to the pub's attraction.

The richly wooded interior is warmed by a huge wood-burning fireplace on the main floor and is visually spacious, featuring high, open-beam ceilings. Adorned with the colourful and unique landscape art of famed local artist E. J. Hughes (1913-2007), it reflects the building's intimate connection with the Cowichan Valley and Vancouver Island. The pub's brewing facility, visible through its glass enclosure, is part of the ambience. The pub's masterful use of limited space was first revealed to the world on its opening in 2006. It has since become a popular destination for locals and visitors alike. Then there is the beer. Like other brew pubs sprouting throughout the Island, this is a setting for those who appreciate the amber elixir.

The "Tool Box," a sampling of four of the pub's regular craft beers plus a seasonal offering (which for me was an excellent wheat beer), lets you enjoy a comparative experience. Cow Bay Lager, Arbutus Ale, Shawnigan Irish Ale and Mount Prevost Porter, sampled together, allow for a genuine appreciation of the differences between brews and a more than satisfying imbibing experience. This is good stuff. Entertainment features Sunday-afternoon music jams as well as weekend entertainment. Just Jake's, the adjacent family restaurant, allows families to enjoy all the food and beverage fare of a pub/restaurant operation that takes price in both its brews and accompanying cuisine.

The menu even includes celiac-friendly fare. The pub has embraced the concept of environmental responsibility in the whole operation. That sense of social responsibility extends to offering complimentary shuttle service on Friday and Saturday evenings. To get a visual sampling of the pub, you can take a virtual tour on the website at craigstreet.ca. Beer aficionados will appreciate the ability to arrange, on request, tours of the brewing facility

Earning your beer
Park conveniently in downtown Duncan and visit the Tourism Cowichan Centre at 135 Third Street (250-746-1099) for local information and maps. Your can casually experience the Totem Pole Walk, incorporating more than 80 poles carved by the Cowichan First Nation people, savour treats at the Saturday farmer's market and enjoy historic old Duncan, of which the Craig Street Brew Pub is very much a part.

ESTABLISHMENT 2 9

The Riverside Inn
56 North Shore Road, Lake Cowichan
1-250-749-4398
Services – wi-fi and wheelchair-accessible. No wheel chair-accessible washrooms

Location
Centre of the town of Lake Cowichan, alongside the Cowichan River.

What makes the Riverside Inn unique: history, setting, family friendly and two riverside patios.

A river runs by it. And has been doing so for over 130 years. This historic edifice has graced the shoreline of the Cowichan River since it opened as a trading post in 1884. Falling victim to fire, it was rebuilt in the early 1900s as a hotel, with major renovations being done in the 1940s. Today it is a much-renovated hotel, pub and liquor store complex that keeps a foot in its history even with an updated decor. The pub gives off a logging mill atmosphere with its heavy wood accents and historic photos reflecting Lake Cowichan's long identification with the logging industry—photos many of the older clientele can relate to personally.

The inn sports two atmosphere-rich patios overlooking the river, one for smokers and the other non-smokers. Here you can enjoy a beer and watch passing life on the river. Boats, kayakers and rafters bring the river to life in season. Indoors, two levels provide venues for entertainment, dancing, pool, and the enjoyment of homemade pub food and refreshments from 10 taps. Craft beers Phillips and Stanley Park share the beer listings with Labatt products.

Entertainment every Friday and Saturday features local talent, when available, as well as DJ music and acoustic performances. Come June, the Inn is an active participant in the annual Lake Days Festival.

The spacious confines, which permit children to accompany parents until 8 p.m., accommodate 188 inside and patio seating for 48 and 100, respectively. At its age, the Riverside has stories to tell. The touching tale of long-time resident and patron "George," for example, for whom a special chair was made. There are those who are uneasy sitting in the chair.

Then there is the enigmatic chair in the attic: too big to get through the door. No one knows how it got there, but it is considered ill luck to move it. Bad things happen. So, does the Riverside have ghosts? Who knows?

The Inn is blessed with good bus service to Duncan, Youbou, Mesachie Lake and Honeymoon Bay, plus a local taxi. Great for those wishing to enjoy a few pints but not to drive afterward.

Here, on a lazy summer day, it is easy to sit back with a brew on one of the patios, watching the life on the river and contemplating how someone might well have been doing the same thing some 100-plus years before.

Earning your beer

From river to forest to town, there is much to do here. Check out ork-aadventures.com and cowichanriver.com for information on river rafting rentals, drop-offs and pick-ups. Drive seven kilometres east on the road to Duncan for the turnoff to Skutz Falls and access to the Trans Canada Trail. There are enough hiking/biking trails in the area to occupy more than a day and work up a healthy thirst and appetite. You can even pick up the Trans Canada Trail (also known locally as the Cowichan Valley Trail) right across the road from the inn.

For trail details, it can be helpful to pick up a map of the Cowichan Valley.

ESTABLISHMENT 30

The Shoe Pub

9576 Chemainus Road, Chemainus
1-250-416-0411
Webpage – horseshoebay-inn.com
Services – wi-fi – wheelchair-accessible with wheel chair-accessible washroom

Location
At the roundabout connecting Henry Road, accessed off Island Highway #1, with Chemainus Road.

What makes the Shoe unique: history, hauntings, and architecture.

The sign says "established 1892," yet the walls of the Horseshoe Inn claim stories from long before. The building and pub have grown up with Chemainus, or perhaps it is the other way around. The original builder, Matthew Howe, first came to these shores from England to install and operate machinery at the mill, but eventually left the mill to build the inn and take up land for farming. No date for the first building remains on record after all these years, but in 1883 the inn, then called Croft and Severne's, received a liquor licence on the grounds that there was "nothing else between Maple Bay and Nanaimo."

The Inn began life as a posting house for horses and carriages travelling the island and as a refuge for visiting sailors and loggers. Needless to say, its early years were colourful. One sad story has left its scar upon a grown tree in the backyard. There, a black bear was chained and challenged to wrestle by alcohol-emboldened patrons, until one day the

bear broke the arm of an adversary and was put down. The chain marks still ring the old tree.

But! The inn also had its years of refinement when managed by Emily Collyer, once in the immediate employ of Queen Victoria, who set a fine table and had her walls adorned with signed photos of the monarch and assorted other images of European aristocracy. And here, too, can be found the signatures of John D. Rockefeller and Dale Carnegie on the register, in the year 1900, as well as the names of famed First Nations poet Pauline Johnson and Western writer Zane Grey.

Then there are other guests. Shadows, they have been called. Shadows caught out of the corner of the eye. Shadows that move things, play non-existent pianos, walk the hallways, turn on radios and TVs, play poltergeist on occasion, or manifest themselves as the sounds of children at play or a meowing cat. Some say there is the ghost of a onetime owner reluctant to depart his former haunts, or the unsettled spirits of two Japanese men murdered there by a racist mob. Whatever the source, the spirits are said to be friendly.

This heritage inn encompasses 10 vintage hotel rooms, a tastefully renovated restaurant, a cold beer and wine store, and a welcoming pub. The wooded pub with its bar faced in tin plate incorporates two raised daises in the main room, plus a pool room behind the bricked gas fireplace. Historic photos of the inn adorn the walls, and the restaurant entrance is graced with an impressive wall mural of the old hotel.

A tended lawn/patio expanse within sight of the Mount Brenton Golf Course affords patrons a breath of fresh air and tranquility, plus a space for contented pooches to rest within sight of their owners. Local fare on the nine taps includes Chemainus' own Riot brewery and Merridale cider, joining three more craft beers and draft Guinness. All complemented by a full bar offering of alcoholic beverages. On Friday and Saturday nights, an in-house DJ entertains the patrons.

"The Shoe" has seen the door swing both ways for many years, years that have seasoned it and made it a core part of Chemainus. Within its walls rest many stories and more than a little mystery.

Earning your beer

Did I already mention the scenic Mount Brenton Golf Course? A nearby treat for visiting swingers. To work up a sweat, you can trek the four-kilometre Rotary Trail, which runs from the far south end of the golf course up to Cook Street, passing right behind the Shoe in the process. Along the way you can explore the Hermit's Trail (once the haunt of Charlie Abbott, whose enigmatic mural can be found near the secret garden off Willow Street) or wander beside meandering Askew Creek, in its namesake park, under an old-growth canopy. You may want to take in a world-class live performances at the Chemainus Theatre (chemainustheatrefestival.ca) or experience the famed mural tour (map available at the tourist information centre). Truth is, for the town's size, there is a lot to see and do here. For more ideas, check out the information centre in its new digs beside the museum in the central town parking lot. (chemainus.bc.ca).

ESTABLISHMENT 31

The Sawmill Taphouse

101B, 3055 Oak Street, Chemainus
                    1-250-324-0222
Website –   sawmilltaphouse.com
Services –   wi-fi, wheelchair-accessible with
                    wheelchair-accessible washrooms

Location
Chemainus Village Square at Oak and Chemainus Road

What makes the Sawmill Taphouse unique: host of beers on tap, interior decor

With a historic sawmill atmosphere and more beer choices than one can address in just a couple of visits, the Sawmill Taphouse & Grill compels visitors to return time and again. The owners take great pride in having the "best" patio in the area and also offer an excellent new events venue.

Stepping into the Sawmill is like taking a walk into the sawmill-centred pioneering days of Vancouver Island. Reclaimed materials have been garnered from old mills throughout the Island and reworked into the floor, ceiling, walls, bar and decor (attested to by the huge milling blades adorning the walls, a floor-to-ceiling photograph mural of a mill interior, and brass castings). One bar beam was salvaged from the Island's first mill, the Somas Mill in Port Alberni. An element not to be ignored is the pair of ornate chandeliers.

Twenty-six taps hold regular fare beers, primarily frm Island craft breweries, including Phillips, Longwood,

Hoyne, Driftwood, and Chemainus' own Riot, plus an ever changing retinue representing other craft breweries. In a nod to the Mainland, Vancouver's 49th Parallel is also included. Four more taps are turned to ciders, including Cowichan's own Merridale, and one to local wines. Seasonal and exotic beers punctuate the offerings, including stouts, Hefeweizens, chocolate porter, and more, plus beverages fragrant with the essences of grapefruit, berries, cloves, melons, orange, lemongrass, caramel and honey. Alcohol levels can range from a high 7.2% to a temperate 3.5%. And all this is in a constant state of flux, offering new experiences for every visit.

It is no wonder three-glass sampler flights for wine, beer, and ciders are popular. There is so much to experience. Ample seating at the bar, booths, tables and outdoor patio provides for almost 150 souls. The superior glassed-in patio option, looking out on Askew Park and a cultivated roundabout, is usually open between mid-May and mid-September. Drawing on a market from Victoria to Parksville, the Sawmill prides itself on being a food-first restaurant reflecting support for local and Island producers. Of particular pride are their burgers and stone-fired pizzas. The Sawmill is living proof of the vitality of Vancouver Island's craft brewing industry and the richness of local product.

<u>Earning your Beer</u>
The Sawmill shares ready access to the four-kilometre Rotary Trail with its neighbour Riot Brewing, but is also within sight of the small but impressive little enclave that is Askew Park. Here Askew Creek, which can be quite dramatic through winter and spring, winds through old stands of rainforest, easily transporting visitors out of their urban world. Like Dr. Who's Tardis, it seems larger on the inside than outside.

For a special treat, consider taking in the famous, live Chemainus Theatre, or doing the walking Mural Tour. Information on the latter and more can be obtained from the tourist information centre in the main parking lot on Willow Street.

ESTABLISHMENT 32

Riot Brewing Company

101A, 3055 Oak Street, Chemainus
                                    1-250-324-7468
Webpage —   riotbrewing.com
Features —   wi-fi, wheelchair-accessible with wheel
                                    chair-accessible washroom

Location
In Chemainus Village Square at Oak Street and Chemainus Road.

What makes Riot Brewing unique: dog-friendly, and its own unique
brewery product

You have to love a place that makes room for dogs and children while
you enjoy a brew, and Riot Brewing is just such a place. It took seven
long years to get the brewery off the ground, and original plans to lo-
cate in Duncan proved futile. The whole operation was in danger of
being located outside the Cowichan area when an encouraging hand
from the North Cowichan Municipality raised the prospect of locating
in the new shopping centre in Chemainus. The result: in 2016 Chemainus got its own community-oriented brewery, owned by co-found-
ers Aly Tomlin, Ralf Rosenke, and Morgan Moreira.

Riot is running hard to keep up with demand for its products, which include five beers on tap, with a different featured seasonal every month.

Patrons can choose from
a variety of ales and la-
gers, with alcohol con-
tent ranging from 6% to
a modest 3.8%, in four-
glass "sampler" flights,
pints, or for takeaway in
refillable growlers, cans
or bottles. In addition

to dispensing low-alcohol beer there are plans to provide a shuttle service.

The modern building has a capacity of 54, accommodated at bar and tables, plus 45 on the outside patio, which is warmed by a fire pit and overlooks the public square, with its gurgling fountain and gardens. Food services are not a feature of Riot, though patrons are offered a copy of the Sawmill Taphouse's offerings, which can be delivered, or they may bring their own food or nibbles. Thanks to this, Riot can be dog-friendly. Here is a place you can bring the family (and perhaps enjoy one of the board games on hand), or your pooch, or both. It truly makes for a comfortable community setting.

That atmosphere is further enhanced by an ongoing range of events. Every second Tuesday is a musical "Ruby Tuesday Jam Night"; once a month there is an open mike, and in between the pub brings in comedians and magicians, puts on fundraisers, and creates sponsorships, all attesting to the owners' philosophy of being an active part of the community. Add to this support for local artists by displaying their works for sale on the walls. A welcome addition to Chemainus, Riot Brewing is already drawing many new visitors to town and actively engaging with the local community.

Earning your beer
Riot shares with its neighbour, the Sawmill Taphouse, proximity to the four-kilometre Rotary Trail, which runs alongside the railway north to Cook Street and south past Mount Brenton Golf Course, almost to Crozier Road. Good for hiking or biking, the trail also offers a side trip to the nearby Hermit Trail, he legacy of the hermit Charlie Abbott, who carved out a series of garden pathways winding through the forest.

It is a short jaunt downtown to the tourist information centre, in the main parking lot, where you can get information on the walking tour of the famed historical murals, the renowned live theatre and more.

ESTABLISHMENT 33

The Saltair Pub

10519 Knight Road, Saltair, V0R 1K2

1-250-246-4942

Services – wi-fi, wheelchair-accessible, no wheelchair-accessible washroom

Location
About four kilometres north of Chemainus and six kilometres south of Ladysmith, on Chemainus Road; well signposted.

What makes the Saltair unique: setting, theme, history, and haunting (?)

Set pastorally amid forest, lawn and field (where once tulips were grown for market), the elegant farm home dating to 1900, when the Porter family set up shop on 80 acres, lost none of its familial charm when it was converted to a pub in 1982. Its owners have included the Knight family, the namesake of the tree-shaded access road. The pub's exterior includes an extensive patio with an open gazebo (for smokers) and a beanbag toss area.

The wood-panelled interior is adorned with antique photos of the English countryside, an extensive collection of old English horse brass, intriguing knickknacks such as model ships, and photos, along with a written and photographic history of the farmhouse. Captions speak of an earlier time when fish ran up the creek, of swimming in the nearby ocean, and of the wealth of produce and livestock once tended by a pioneering family. All serve to create a homey atmosphere, especially when

rain is pattering down on a winter's eve and the rock-faced fireplace is ablaze.

Patrons can play darts, watch TVs typically tuned to sports, and enjoy subtle background music while seated around the bar or at separate tables. Service includes taps leaning heavily to Island craft beers, including Phillips (Victoria), Hoyne (Victoria), Riot Brewery of Chemainus, and Merridale Cider (Cowichan), accompanied by Guinness—plus a full menu.

There is word the farmhouse is haunted by an apparition simply known as the Lady in the Blue Dress, whose origins are unknown but whose presence is benign. Not much of a surprise, given the many years and the many people who have passed the doors of this farmhouse.

<u>Earning your beer</u>
Two kilometres north of the pub, on Chemainus Road, is a small blue signpost marking the way to Stocking Creek Trail and its small parking lot. This hilly and winding trail, with an upper section and a lower section hugging the creek, stretches along two kilometres as the crow flies and offers the riches of a rainforest walk plus a scenic waterfall thrown in. It also runs alongside a portion of the broader Trans Canada Trail, which can be picked up at the opposite end of the parking lot and trekked a distance farther north.

ESTABLISHMENT 34

Fox & Hounds British Pub Style Restaurant

11 High Street, Ladysmith

1-250-924-1747

Webpage – foxandhoundsladysmith.com

Services – wi-fi, wheelchair-accessible with wheelchair-accessible washrooms

<u>Location</u>
High Street off of First Avenue. Angle parking.

<u>What makes the Fox & Hounds unique:</u> British theme, history, beer range

Dr. Who fans know that what you see on the outside does not indicate what you find on the inside. The new Fox & Hounds in Ladysmith is the surprise box of candy.

Painstaking efforts to create a British-style pub in atmosphere and form have been successfully achieved by the owners, who also brought us the unique Black Goose, south of Parksville. Though the faux-paned windowed exterior of the pub leads you to expect a simple contemporary interior, that thought is dispelled the minute you gaze in the window or open the door.

You are greeted with Tudor-style half-timbered decor befitting Henry VIII. Pass into the inner sanctum to find more of the same, on a grander scale. The personal tankards of regular patrons hang as adornment, lending a community familiarity to the place, and the rewards of "tegestology" fill the rafters. Original wood floors, dating back to the

many years the building served as a hardware store, are now overseen by half-timbered walls and an open-beam ceiling. The spacious arrangement for seating ranges from single bar stools to tables and chairs. Antique furniture graces the corners, with the promise of more on the way. A lone piano occupies a spot at the back wall with an open invitation for those so talented to tickle the ivories. One would be hard-pressed to recognize that the building began life in 1890 as a blacksmith's forge before being turned into a hardware store in the 1940s.

Cozy up to the bar and you can pick between four taps, including the products of Nanaimo's Longwood Brewpub. The beer aficionado's palate will be more than well served with the additional 12 imported beers on tap. These include one of Oktoberfest's official brewery products: Hacker-Pschorr Weisse, which is served with formal ritual befitting the standards of its Bavarian heritage. To this, for full Orwellian pleasure, add draft Guinness. Nor is this a parlour-sized pub. It accommodates 144 patrons, when you include a theme-consistent private room and spacious outdoor patio at the back.

As a food-service-primary outlet, the pub welcomes children at all times. English fare dominates the menu, and ordering for both food and beverage is done at the bar. Bus service information is available via ladysmith.ca/our-services/ladysmith-transit.

The Fox & Hounds has managed to capture the uniqueness of a themed pub and complement it with a casual style of welcome. Makes you want to use the British phone box out front to tell all your friends about it.

Earning your beer
Here in the heart of Ladysmith, there is a host of things to see and do: antique shops abound, you can enjoy live theatre, and in season there's the spectacular Ladysmith Light Up, when the main street comes ablaze with lights for Christmas.

But to work up an appetite and thirst, there is the worthy challenge of the Holland Creek and Heart Lake Trails, with a trailhead not far away. In season, the gurgle of the stream becomes an ominous roar as Holland Creek

tumbles down to join the salt chuck. Its 5.8 kilometres, one way, are a healthy clamber, bottom to top, but along the way the path offers rewarding views of Crystal Falls and the Colliery Dams. At the crest of the hike is a more strenuous scramble farther on to the secluded setting of Heart Lake, which offers breathtaking views over ocean and island.

Information and maps are online at tourismladysmith.ca. The site suggests further hiking options in the area. Family-friendly Transfer Beach is alive with activity during the summer, with sponsored events, music, and kayak rentals. For more, check out the information centre at 33 Robert St. (250-245-2112) or email admin@ladysmithcofc.com, or visit the website ladysmithcofc.com.

SECTION THREE The Gulf Islands

ESTABLISHMENT 35

The Hummingbird Pub

47 Sturdies Bay Road, Galiano Island
1-250-539-5472
Webpage –   hummingbirdpub.com
Services –   wi-fi, wheelchair-accessible with
                    wheelchair-accessible washroom

Location
A half-hour walk from the ferry at Sturdies Bay, along Sturdies Bay Road

What makes the Hummingbird unique: location, setting, decor, atmosphere, family-friendly, menu

Some pubs begin with flair and exhibit all the modern-day features beloved of a large market drawn to such elements. Others evolve and, while doing so, authentically display their legacy of many changes wrought by time and circumstance, so that their story is apparent the moment you approach the door.

Such is the Hummingbird Pub of Galiano Island.
For over 20 years, owner Debbie Spees has nurtured her Island gathering place of socializing and song with all the industriousness of its namesake. A place that embraces the outdoors, with its sheltered deck and sunroom bathed in light, as much as the indoors. A pool room, central seating area (replete with church-pew bench seating), a bar with stool seating, and the snug (a cozy lower-level seating hollow wrapped around

a wood-burning fireplace) make the indoors a welcoming comfort.

The sunroom gleams under its skylights, enhancing the colour of hanging banners. The intimacy of the snug is heightened by sunlight pouring through a stained-glass hummingbird window, which brings to life the compelling flower and hummingbird mural by local artist Keith Holmes that sprawls across the hearth and wall. Paintings by local artists are also displayed. Outside, real hummingbirds rally round bird feeders, embellishing an already inviting setting of garden, forest and light. Each section of the pub offers a slightly different atmosphere and ample room for patrons to pick their preference for intimate, individual, or group seating.

Family-friendly, the pub has a children's activity zone set up just below the outer deck, as well as seating for parents who are keeping an eye on their little ones. Extra services include wi-fi and a seasonal bus service driven by Island renowned "Tommy," famed for entertaining patrons in the course of their journey to and from the Island marina at Montague Harbour and the adjacent provincial park—a trip worth the experience alone. The service has been running, seasonally, for over 30 years, beginning on the May long weekend and operating full time from mid-June to the last week in September.

From May to September, live entertainment is provided on Friday and Saturday nights. The beer taps rotate; Guinness and Aderley and Avril Creek wines from Vancouver Island are also included. Of particular pride are the Hummingbird "pies" famed among the Islanders. Add to this a mostly gluten-free menu, a large vegetarian menu, and produce from the owners' own Hummingbird Farms. From the moment you pass by the greeting gargoyle at the door till you climb aboard the return bus, you can savour the essence of all things Galiano. It's easy to see why the well-travelled hummingbirds wing back here, as do many patrons who, having once found this haven, return to its welcoming comfort.

Earning your beer
For those whose affections run to hiking, you can begin earning a refreshing elixir by hiking the Sturdies Bay Trail, which begins just past Burrill Road at Sturdies Bay Road and takes you all the way to the Hummingbird. The half-hour trek, which skirts Sturdies Bay Road, offers a side hike to Bluff Park, one of the numerous regional and provincial parks on the island. Ample hiking trails dot the island, and it is also a regular attraction for cycling groups. Both groups frequent the Hummingbird in season. Shore access points are numerous on the south island, which takes pride in being a major destination for birders, with 150 winged species frequenting the area. Check out galianoisland.com and pick up a Galiano Island map available on the ferry.

ESTABLISHMENT 36

The Springwater Lodge Pub

Miners Bay, Mayne Island

1-250-539-5521

Webpage – springwaterlodge.com

Services – wi-fi, wheelchair-accessible

Location
At the head of Miner's Bay, a 40-minute walk from the ferry dock if you want to do a visit a la feet, otherwise a five-minute drive.

What makes the Springwater unique: view, location, setting, history and hauntings (?)

The Springwater claims to be the oldest licensed lodge in British Columbia, having begun its reign in 1892. Miner's Bay was a favoured stop for Fraser River and Caribou Gold Rush miners on their way to the mainland in the late 1850s and had settlers putting down roots as early as 1859. Initially built as a residence, the lodge began offering rooms in 1895 as the Grandview Lodge, and its rustic form has graced the shoreline ever since.

Still offering five rental rooms in the summer, the lodge keeps its taps open all year in its heritage building. It carries its age, obviously, but very well, and in so doing enhances its appeal.

The pub, which dates from the late 1950s, occupies the main floor and opens out upon a wide deck with a magnificent vista spanning Active Pass and encompassing Galiano Island. BC Ferries ships trundle past, sharing space with sailboats and power craft. Occasionally a black dorsal fin breaks the surface to signal passing orcas. In their honour, a wood carving of an orca graces the side deck. The pub has one central room, an entertainment room with TV, a pool table and a cozy free-standing fireplace for damp nights, to complement the wide deck. Wood wainscotting with a carpeted floor, a wood ceiling and clean lines characterize the central pub. Adjacent to the pub and deck is the restaurant, which is a tad more fancy, with wood wainscotting, ornate wallpaper and historical photos.

Word has it a friendly lady ghost, believed by some to be that of former owner Emma Maylor, who died in 1952, still walks the halls. Tales also tell of a former cook who still frequents the kitchen.
Sitting on the deck watching the failing light of sunset, it is easy to drift away and feel as if you are one of those miners of bygone days, dreaming of gold even as the peaceful setting washes over you.

Earning your beer
 Within a 30-minute trek along the paved Fernhill Road to Montrose is the trailhead for paths through Mount Parke Park, which connects with Plumper Pass Community Park; both offer up views over the Gulf Islands. Numerous beach access points dot Mayne Island, complemented by more hiking trails, all of which are outlined on visitor guide maps available at the information booth near the Village Bay ferry terminal.

Georgina Point Heritage Park and Lighthouse is a short drive or bike ride from Miner's Bay and provides for grand views, on a clear day, of the distant Vancouver skyline. For birders, Active Pass is an identified Important Bird Area that supports 40 species of marine birds, best observed between August and spring (conservancyonmayne.com).

In addition to regular forms of travel, Mayne, like some other Gulf Islands, has hitchhiking stations, reflecting the laid-back island atmosphere.

ESTABLISHMENT 37

The Port Browning Pub

Port Browning, North Pender Island
1-250-629-3493
Webpage – portbrowning.com
Services – wi-fi, wheelchair-accessible with wheelchair-accessible washroom

Location
On the water at the end of Hamilton Road, which cuts off to the left on Canal Road just after you pass the Driftwood shopping centre heading south.

What makes the Port Browning Pub unique: setting, view, location, history, the totem pole and beach
Blessings for a place may come in many forms and from unexpected sources.

Back when Lucille "Lou" Henshaw and her family acquired this seemingly ill-fated restaurant and property in 1975 and began the long battle to open it as a pub (in 1977), she was inspired to get a four-foot-tall totem pole as central feature. With such in mind, she headed for north Vancouver Island. Chance had her stop in Duncan, where she laid eyes on the work of the yet unheralded Coast Salish sculptor Simon Charlie. With Simon's encouragement, the four-foot pole became a 12-foot house pole, and it was brought to Pender by the master carver himself, sealing a long-standing friendship between him and Lou. The mosquito-adorned bear eating a fish remains the pub's central feature, and Simon Charlie, now passed on (1920–2005),

is famed throughout the world for his carvings, which are on display at the Royal B.C. Museum, the Parliament Buildings in Ottawa, and in international galleries and collections. Among the numerous awards bestowed on Hwunumets, his Salish name, was the Order of Canada.

Though moved amid dramatic pub renovations, The Totem remains a central feature of the spacious interior, housed under high, open ceilings and warmed by a wealth of windows and skylights that allow the light and vista to flood into the two-tiered interior. A partial wrap-around deck opens to an unimpeded view of Mount Norman and the distant rise of Orcas Island in the U.S. The long, sheltered arm of the bay focuses the eyes on the island-scaped horizon, while becalmed waters allow boats to ride quietly at anchor and the occasional great blue heron to swoop by, low and silent.

Long known by the name Sha-Qua-Ala Inn, literally translated as The Watering Hole, its acquisition by new owners has led to greater prominence for the Port Browning Pub. In keeping with the new ownership, renovations have touched all parts of the marina complex, including the pub, cafe (now the Bridgewater Bistro) and marina. The atmospheric history of the pub has not been forgotten, as attested to by the humorous plate work of Ralph Sketch, a well-known local artist, titled

"Home from the Pub" and featuring a happy man on horseback, beer stein in hand, galloping freely. It rests above the gas fireplace, one of two featured at the inn, the second being a wood-burning type. A photo from the cover of Pacific Yachting Magazine, circa the '90s, features an aerial view of the pub and marina, and the old bar mantel hangs above the second fireplace. More important, founder and past owner Lou, now in her eighties, continues to visit.

The two-tiered interior is spacious and incorporates both bar seating and tables and chairs, plus an entertainment niche with a pool table. The resort itself includes the marina, camping, restaurant, pub, and swimming pool, and has its own broad beach. Local live entertainment occasionally blesses hearth and home, particularly in the summer months, and the 10 rotating taps give a nod to Vancouver Island craft beers, offering the products of Hoyne, Driftwood, Phillips, and Lighthouse breweries of Victoria, to complement a local cider.

The spacious grounds and beach accommodate special events such as the New Year's Polar Bear Swim, the 20-year-old annual Frisbee tourney, the cardboard boat race, and car shows.
The Port Browning Pub remains quietly blessed by its totem, thus keeping a toe in the past even as it remodels for the future. A welcoming feature for its long-loyal patrons.

Earning your beer
On site are kayak rentals and tours to complement the swimming beach. A short drive away is part of the Gulf Islands National Park Reserve. The Heart Trail there connects to other trails, eventually leading to the renowned Frisbee golf course (the Golf Island Disc Park). The national park offers overnight (one night only) camping, and the disc golf grounds are guaranteed to keep you fit, just running about over the hills and rocks flinging your Frisbee.

The longest island hike, which provides for excellent viewpoints, is Mount Norman on South Pender. It carries you to a height of 244 metres, and it takes between 30 and 45 minutes to reach the summit.

There is also the Pender Island Golf & Country Club, the Saturday farmer's market, running from mid-April to mid-October, and the Pender Island Museum, for those wishing to embrace the local ambience. A nice travel feature are the hitchhiking car stops dotted about the island.

Check out Penderisland.info and hellobc.com/pender-islands

ESTABLISHMENT **38**

Saturna Lighthouse Pub

100 East Point Road

	1-250-539-5725
Webpage –	saturnapub.com
Services –	wi-fi, wheelchair-accessible

Location
Can't miss it if you come by ferry or boat to Lyall Harbour. It sits on your immediate right at the ferry berth, perched upon the rocks. Parking on site and angle parking close by, up the road.

What makes the Lighthouse Pub unique: setting, location and especially the view
Perched on the edge of the sea, the Lighthouse Pub and Restaurant is as perfectly set up for sunsets as Stonehenge. Green-clad islands surround the lapping waters, cormorants dry themselves on the dock, accompanied by complaining gulls, and sharp white sails play and traverse the waters—sounds and sights as calming as they are mesmerizing.

The Lighthouse Pub has known more stability than some; its present owners have been holding the fort since 2007, and the previous ones ran it for over 20 years. The pub is part of a complex, called The Point, involving a marina, gas service, convenience store, bike rental and repair shop, and an art gallery. There is also a new campground across the road: Arbutus Point Campground. The complex's broad arms span both sides of the ferry dock. The pub offers a central room, with table and chair seating to accompany bar seating along the 25-foot cedar bar, and a spectacular deck. A pel-

photo courtesy Krystine Hogan)

let stove helps warm the winters, and light pours through the large windows, offering patrons a view even when weather chases them indoors. To while away cool nights, there are board games and darts, while the adjacent cubbyhole can and has been altered for specialized activities.

The restaurant has its own table-and-chair room and an outdoor patio to rival the pub's. Outside deck banister seating gives patrons a 180-degree view. By chance, the favoured Vancouver Island craft beer on tap is none other than Victoria's own Lighthouse Brewery, a matter of coincidence rather than design. Great pride is taken in the fish and chips, which can be savoured next to the sea.

Whether you find yourself sitting on the deck basking in a stunning sunset or enjoying cozy warmth on a cool day, this is a pub that exudes a sense of calm and community, on an ungentrified island that retains the feel of an older time.

Earning your beer
You don't have to go far from the pub to enjoy a unique experience. The Wild Thyme Coffee House is a can't-miss experience, be it for treats, coffee, or atmosphere. Housed in an old double-decker bus, it has a kitchen downstairs, with seating upstairs or outside in the open seating area. It's only a hop, skip, and jump from the pub centre, in which the Prism art gallery, run by international artist Janet Strayer, is worth checking out.

A healthy 20-minute walk will get you to the island's general store, which recollects much earlier times. This unpressured jewel of the Gulf Islands is rich in places to hike and bike, such as nearby Mount Warburton Pike, which can be reached by road and has numerous lead-off trails. Parks regional and provincial complement the large Gulf Islands National Park Reserve, which owns much of the centre of the island and is but one part of numerous reserve sites spread about the southern Gulf Islands.

(photo courtesy Saturna Pub)

Check out the activities of

Saturna Island Marine Research and Education Society, or SIMRES (saturnamarineresearch.ca). Their interactive presentations bring the seascape to life. Captain Larry Peck is up on all things Saturna.

And keep an eye out on the waters, an easy thing to do with the many viewpoints on the island, for the entertainment can be sudden, unexpected and breathtaking. And it is not orcastrated!
Pick up an island brochure and map from the ferry or at the pub. Also, check out saturnatourism.com.

The Islands are not a place to come and experience in a hurry, and nowhere is this more true than on Saturna. Note: A special feature of the island is the free Saturna shuttle bus run by the Lions. Its schedule is posted at the ferry dock.

ESTABLISHMENT 39

Shipstone Taproom and Lounge

110 Purvis Lane, #201, Ganges, Salt Spring Island
1-250-537-5041
Webpage – saltspringtakeout.com/oystercatcher
Services – wi-fi, wheelchair-accessible with wheelchair-accessible washrooms

Location
In the heart of Ganges, overlooking the bay and alongside the boardwalk.

What makes the Shipstone unique: setting, location, atmosphere

The chameleon's colour tells you the season. In winter, the Shipstone's cozy confines, warmed by a gas fireplace, invite the patron in from the damp. In summer, the doors come off to embrace sun and sea, spilling an appreciative clientele out onto the harbour's margin. This practice has been going on for 15 years under the present ownership.

The Shipstone Taproom and Lounge is part of the greater Oystercatcher restaurant complex, which has a separate restaurant above and taproom below. Hovering over the water world of harbour and marina, it is part of Ganges' busy hive.

The winter-enclosed seating accommodates 45 with tables, sofas and

bar seating in a modern, trendy setting fitted for sports watching and proximate for chat. Come summer, the inside and outside become indistinguishable, and a further 180 bottoms can be accommodated. The upstairs restaurant accommodates 90 more.

Nestled beside the boardwalk rimming the harbour, and seasonally extended with outdoor heating and two outdoor fireplaces, the pub offers days and nights, May to September, for atmosphere appreciation. Regular performers Simone or Mike Demers provide popular nightly outdoor entertainment that adapts to the audience. Enjoy your meal and refreshment, listen to music, and watch the sun play out its dance over the bay.

Priding itself on its menu and beverages, the Shipstone owns 10 beer taps and includes Salt Spring Island Brewery products as feature brews, along with Guinness. Uniquely, one tap is devoted to prosecco, an Italian sparkling wine drawn from prosecco grapes primarily grown in the Veneto region of Italy. Complementing this are bellinis—a cocktail composed of prosecco and peach puree or nectar.

If seeking a quiet respite during the day, a patron can lounge on an Adirondack chair and watch the busy little harbour for endless entertainment. Float planes come and go (regular service to Victoria, Vancouver and Nanaimo), a great blue heron rises gracefully from the shore, watercraft big and small arrive and depart, and the light plays upon water and forest—this is a place for appreciative reflection. Whatever the season, the chameleon's colours are always inviting.

Earning your beer

The Shipstone is blessed with long-term staff knowledgeable about what there is to see and do in Ganges and on Salt Spring. Hiking or biking the nearby trails of Mount Erskine and Mount Maxwell will more than build a thirst and appetite, as well as open up grand vistas (islandpathways.ca). The Frisbee golf course is within walking distance, and the summer Saturday farmers market is widely renowned. A visit to the tourist information centre, which sits above the central Ganges parking lot, off the main road through town, will fill your mitts with brochures and maps on what there is to see and do.

Bus service is provided to all three ferry terminals as well as the Ganges area (bctransit/region/saltspringislandsystem). It is worthwhile checking out funky Fulford Harbour village to rekindle that '60s and '70s feel.

ESTABLISHMENT 40

Moby's Pub

124 A Upper Ganges Road, Salt Spring Island
1-250-537-5559
Webpage –   mobyspub.ca
Services –   wi-fi, wheelchair-accessible with
                  wheelchair-accessible washrooms

Location
Immediately adjacent to the town of Ganges, off the road to Long Harbour. Salt Spring Island and Ganges are well served by ferries from Vancouver, Victoria and Crofton, by the island's community bus, and by float plane air service by Salt Spring Air and Harbour Air. For the boat people, there is direct access to the pub from the marina.

What makes Moby' s unique: view, location, architecture, setting and historical features
Moby's, a name evoking images of the great creatures of the sea, fittingly rests at the head of a bay that has known odd appearances by these denizens of the deep.

Strategically placed at the top of a long arm of Ganges Harbour, Moby's is blessed with a view both contemplative and dynamic. The play of nature's moods and light upon vista and foreshore create an ever-changing artistic scene: the rumbling throb of a float plane clawing its way skyward, a harbour seal's curious cruise, the vibrant overlay of islands

fading to the horizon, all moving in their own time frame, free from the hastened norms of everyday life. Viewed from the glassed-in comfort of the interior or from the outdoor patio, the views are equally captivating.

Moby's came to life as a

pub in 1989, evolving into four different levels, inside and out, centred on the bar, the views, the fireplaces, and a lofty overview of the interior. Bar and table seating accommodate groups and individuals, while the dedicated stage emphasizes the importance here of live entertainment. Well-known Canadian artist and Salt Spring Island resident Valdy has more than once owned the podium.

The present structure, built in 1991 under the ownership of several locals, remained in the same hands until 2003. A plaque commemorates Dick Durante, one of the original owners, and references some of his pearls of wisdom. After 2003, ownership changes came fast and frequent until the present owners took charge in in June 2013 and began returning Moby's to its former glory.

From the open ceiling is suspended handmade kayak constructed from strong but light materials. Other artifacts spotted as you casually toss your glance around include an ancient dory, a forever-cresting blue wooden marlin, and a ukulele-playing wooden hula dancer who owns her own lofty corner.

The taps include Sweet Leaf IPA from Duncan's Red Arrow Brewery and that international favourite, Guinness.
Focussing on food has helped Moby's gain recognition for offering something more than typical "pub fare" cuisine, such as its duck wings done in a chili-soy sauce.

This is a place to dine and drink, but keep an eye on the bay, for you never know what you might see.

Earning Your Beer
This is Salt Spring Island, and the list of things to see and do seems almost inexhaustible. Within easy walking distance of pub and village is the island's disc golf course, an attraction for the Frisbee-tossing population. Nearby, healthy treks up Mount Erskine and Mount Maxwell will more than earn you a beer and throw in magnificent views as a bonus. Biking and hiking trails dot the island (islandpathways.ca). Summertime is busy with the famed summer Saturday market, but vibrant life continues in the off-season with events such as the Harvest Festival in

October, which offers food and drink (wines, meads and beer) with a distinctly local flavour, from farm to vineyard to brewery to menu.

Moby's plays an integral role in the festivities as a contestant and venue for dancing and socializing. Sailing tours, whale-watching expeditions, float plane tours and island water taxi service call Ganges Harbour home base. The off-season affords the riches of the Island and town without the greater press of humanity. Within short driving distance of Ganges are three vineyards, the Salt Spring Brewery, a meadery and Fulford Harbour's funky village, providing clothing and wares harking back to the '60s and '70s, as well as markets reminiscent of the Middle East or Asia.

Christmas on Salt Spring (christmasonsaltspring.com) has become a major annual event, with carolling, food and drink competitions, music, Santa, markets and all that is Christmas.

A visit to the tourist information centre in Ganges provides for maps and printed information, accompanied by the helpful advice of local volunteers.

The community bus service (bctransit/Region/Salt Spring Island System) connects Ganges with all three ferry docks and also offers a Ganges circuit.

ESTABLISHMENT 41

The Local Pub

#108-149 Ganges Road, Ganges, Salt Spring Island
1-250-931-7778
Webpage - saltspringlocalpub.com
Services – wi-fi, wheelchair-accessible with wheelchair-accessible washrooms

Location
At the bottom of Gasoline Alley, overlooking the bay.

What makes The Local unique: view, the location, swans and palm trees

Ganges is a busy tourist town, especially in the summer months, when the press of crowds and the buzz of markets is most prevalent. So, at such times, where do the locals go?
Tucked away in a corner, with its own unimpeded harbour view, sporting an annual visiting swan family and framed by palm trees, rests their most appropriately named refuge, The Local Pub.

A long-time watering hole of greater dimensions, it has been reduced to a cozy venue affording seating for 30 in the window-lit interior, complemented by a further 25 in the glassed-in and awning-covered patio. A wrap-around bar in fine woods surrounded by bar stools is conducive to communal conversation and ease of service. The patio's retractable awning protects from excessive sun or the peril of rain, while letting patrons enjoy the outdoors, with portable heaters extending the season.

The 10 taps are devoted almost entirely to Vancouver Island and Salish Sea offerings, including products from Phillips and Vancouver Island

breweries of Victoria and Salt Spring's own brewery. A separate tap is dedicated to red wine.

Affectionately called The Office by regular patrons because it is a place where personal exchanges occur, this is a pub that lives up to its name.

While tourist season and the famed Saturday market, which surrounds the pub, bring in the visitors, the off-season belongs to the locals.

Fridays see local musical talent, of which plenty abounds on the island, entertaining the masses.
Five screens, tuned largely to sport, are there to keep fans up to date.

Parked out of the way, with its own private screening of harbour life and aura of palm trees, The Local exudes a feeling of warm refuge cherished by locals and bound to be appreciated by respectful visitors.

Earning your beer
Like its compatriots, the Shipstone and Moby's, The Local is a fine accompaniment to the host of activities Salt Spring Island has to offer.

Not too distant is the trail that takes hikers on a healthy jaunt to the summit of Mount Maxwell. From the fenced edge of the viewpoint on top, you can scan the island from north to south, embracing a view over southern Vancouver Island, and watch the tiny maritime traffic far below. Hang-gliders and paragliders frequent the area and you may well spy them riding the air currents like great winged beasts.

It's well worth the hike, or even the rough road drive up.

ESTABLISHMENT 42

Thetis Island Marina & Pub

Telegraph Harbour, Thetis Island
1-250-246-3464
Webpage - thetisisland.com
Services – wi-fi, wheelchair-accessible with wheel chair-accessible washrooms

Location
At Telegraph Harbour on Thetis Island (named in 1851 after the Royal Navy frigate Thetis), about a 15- minute leisurely walk from the BC Ferries dock at Preedy Harbour. Turn right and head toward Foster Point. Harbour Road cuts off to the left and lands you at the pub and marina. Air service to and from Vancouver is offered by SEAIR Seaplanes, while BC Ferries connects with Chemainus on Vancouver Island. (seaairseaplanes.com)

What makes the Thetis Island Pub unique: setting, view, atmosphere, history, eagles

It is difficult to ignore 30 bald eagles all in one place, resting majestically in shoreline trees, hopping along the shoreline, engaging in sharp-taloned courtship, or soaring gracefully on high. So we witnessed them one June at Telegraph Harbour and learned they gather in this way every year.

We took in their show from the outer deck of the Thetis Island Pub while I was having my first experience with homemade yam fries. Both fries and eagles invited further visits.

Former RCAF pilot Paul Deacon operated this

prime island gathering place from 1993 to 2017 and oversaw its evolution as pub, restaurant and marina. The welcome mat is out from morning coffee to meals and barley sandwiches. The comfy interior is warmed by a wood-burning stove and offers a long outer deck enriched by a panorama that sweeps over the marina and harbour. The wooded interior provides ample table and chair seating, with a polished hardwood floor sporting an inlaid compass rose. A music niche offers a spot for jamming and harbours a guitar and piano that anyone who dares is welcome to play. The bright pub's many windows ensure that eyes are never far from the dynamic scene outside. A brew can be savoured from within or outdoors, while enjoying the busy marina, the performing eagles and the comings and goings of sea planes.

The original marina began in the 1940s, with buildings that were floated down the bay and hauled up above the tide line to form the beginnings of the Cassidy General Store and Post Office. In time, a restaurant was added, and in 1986 a licence led to the birth of the pub. Post office and general store services also continue to this day. It's easy to appreciate that this is the island hub for 300-plus "Thetisians," given it offers a convenience store, liquor store, maritime fuelling, post office, sea plane service (three flights per day to Vancouver) and some rental accommodation. It is also wheelchair-friendly and offers wi-fi. Services are expected to be enhanced under the new ownership of Wayne Procter.

A few years back, Paul had a visit from the original builder and owner, who waxed nostalgic about the old days. A few years afterwards, his daughter approached Paul about spreading her father's ashes from the seawall. So it came to pass the pioneer merged with the present and visits forever with the eagles.

An outside picnic and open barbecue area lets patrons grab a pint and take a meal off the pub grounds, thereby to enjoy the company of their favourite pet while imbibing.

The pub taps carry two Vancouver Island craft beers—Phillips Blue Buck and Hoynes—as well as standard fare. A fine single malt Scotch is among the other alcoholic offerings. A full-fare kitchen provides a tasty accompaniment to any brew.

The secluded and peaceful setting has brought a few famous names to the pub over the years, including those of Andrew Lloyd Webber and Julie Andrews.

Like the eagles on their annual pilgrimage, the islanders gather here, but irrespective of season. And in their midst, you can add the eternal presence of the home-coming pioneer.

<u>Earning your beer</u>
The second weekend of May marks the annual island regatta, in which 50 to 60 sail craft race around Thetis and Penelakut Island; 2019 will mark the race's 25th anniversary. Excellent photos of the regatta line the interior walls of the pub.

Some folk come to kayak the waters, passing through the narrow Canoe Pass separating Thetis and Penelakut Islands (dredged in 1905 to allow boat passage), others to explore beaches and hike the island trails and roads, while still others simply come to explore the island and luxuriate in its peacefulness. Quiet, paved roads invite biking, with a couple of high points nearing 600 feet (183 metres), providing a challenge or a sedate walk. Diving operations on the island include 49th Parallel Dive Charters, operating out of the marina.

A helpful visitors' map and guide to Thetis Island is available at the Chemainus ferry dock and at various spots on Thetis. It provides listings of island B&Bs and services.

Check out the island community site at thetisisland.net

ESTABLISHMENT 43

Silva Bay Pub and Restaurant

3383 South Road, Gabriola Island
1-250-247-8662
Webpage - silvabay.com
Services – wi-fi, wheelchair-accessible with wheel
chair-accessible washrooms

Location
At the extreme south end of Gabriola Island, off of South Road. Getting there and back is enhanced by taking Gabriola's bus service provided by "Gertie." The schedule is posted on-site and at gabriolacommunity-bus.com. Mariners have the luxury of the marina, and Tofino Air provides service from Vancouver and Nanaimo.

What makes Silva Bay unique: setting, location, history, view
It is hard to believe, sitting on the deck at the Silva Bay Pub and Restaurant, overlooking this peaceful sheltered bay, that the hive of activity that is Vancouver is just over the horizon. This is the closest crossing point across the Georgia Strait from Vancouver, and it accommodates mariners jumping off to points north and south through the Gulf Islands and to the shores of Vancouver Island.

Silva Bay takes its name from one of the early pioneers. Portuguese-born John Silva allegedly jumped ship in B.C. and eventually settled at the bay, along with his growing family, after taking up an abandoned

homestead in the early 1880s. The site evolved into a small but permanent community. The Silvas donated land for the historic log Catholic church that rose there in the 1920s and still stands.

In 1945, Les Withey, a

self-taught ship builder from Vancouver, moved to the bay with his family and became partners in a shipbuilding operation that remained in his hands until 1974.

Together with wife Marg, he saw the shipyard business grow to include a marina in the 1960s, and its services expanded to include a licensed restaurant and cafe. In 1968, the resort was sold to Silva Bay Resorts, which eventually moved the licensed services up the hill to the pub's present location.

The pub restaurant is blessed with a panoramic deck, where patrons can drink up the view of the bay, its host of visiting craft, and the distant light-halo of hectic Vancouver. The Royal Vancouver Yacht Club sits on its own little island across the bay. The pub's interior, with its high ceiling, allows light and view to flood in through the large windows facing the deck. Local artists' creations on the walls, a gas fireplace enclosed in a floor-to-ceiling brick hearth, and bar seating as well as tables and chairs for groups lend a sense of spaciousness. Eyes are compulsively drawn to the flower-festooned outdoor deck, with its great view. Good weather makes it a natural magnet always popular with patrons.

Great pride is taken in the quality of the menu here, all meals being made from scratch. Vancouver Island craft brewery products are represented by Wolf brewery of Nanaimo and Hoyne brewery from Victoria. And there is always a stout on tap. All eight taps are dedicated to craft beers. Entertainment free of a cover charge is provided Friday and Saturday nights.

This is a seasonal restaurant pub, opening in May and offering patrons its maritime setting until the clock strikes 10 p.m. on Sept. 30. The view from the deck alone is worth a special trip.

Earning your beer
The bay hosts kayak rentals and tour operators, with miles of shoreline and nearby bays to play in. Nearby Drumbeg Provincial Park is home to trails, a kilometre-long sandy beach, protected Garry oak forest, and a host of critters to watch for in their natural environment. Fishing charters operate out of the bay, as does a scuba diving charter operation.

Check gabriolaisland.org for more information.

ESTABLISHMENT 44

The Surf Lodge and Pub

885 Berry Point Road

	1-250-247-9231
Webpage –	surflodgegrabriola.com
Hours –	Noon to 12 a.m. Sunday to Wednesday
	Noon to 1 a.m. Thursday to Saturday
Services -	wi-fi

Location

Take the first left onto Taylor Bay Road after getting off the ferry from Nanaimo. It becomes Berry Point Road. Follow the signs, staying on Berry Point Road, and the Surf will be on your right overlooking Georgia Strait. Community bus "Gertie" (gabriolacommunitybus.com) provides some service and there is reliable taxi service to the ferry terminal.

What makes the Surf Pub unique: view, history, setting, location, garden

If you hear the pounding of the surf rolling quietly in your ears even when you are within the wooded confines of the Surf Pub, you needn't be surprised. Legend has it the pub was built from raw beach-salvaged logs washed ashore back in the 1950s.

A structural part of the older Surf Lodge, built in the 1930s, the pub has experienced many incarnations over the years. In 2015, it began running year-round again after a period when it operated only seasonally. It

strikes the ideal balance between serving tourists and locals and is an integral part of the Lodge and restaurant complex.

The rustic exterior of wood and stone, entered from the frontage parking lot by a cavernous staircase entrance, gives way to a spacious, burnished log interior with high ceilings, looking out on an unobstructed vista of the Georgia Strait. Flooded with natural light from windows and skylights, the place features a rock wall, art pieces, a homey wood stove and a wide range of seating options serving individuals, couples or larger groups. A pool table, darts and big-screen TV have their place as well. An outer deck, with railings and flowers, faces the sea and offers a view warranting the description spectacular. The large front lawn, dotted with picnic tables, accommodates a hundred souls, including dogs and children, while a well-tended garden offers its own little Eden.

A well-travelled visitor on site to produce music videos proclaimed the view comparable to any he has ever seen. The open waters here bless the eyes with a view of the coastal islands and the towering, glacial peaks of the Coast Mountain range. Passing cruise ships and BC Ferries ships are joined by pods of orcas and fishing boats chasing herring runs, capped off in the evening by stunning sunsets—nightly shows as dramatic in the quiet winter season as in the heady days of summer. As if to make the grandeur of nature even more reachable, a family of swallows had taken up residence above a doorway during our visit, tiny heads peeking out on occasion to survey the greater world.

Fittingly, the 10 beer taps include Vancouver Island products from Driftwood and Hoyne (Victoria), as well as Nanaimo's Longwood.
On Thursday evenings, there's a longstanding tradition of a music jam with John Gresham. This Surf-infused and homey lodge, time- and weather-worn, warrants a special trip to experience this embrace of sea and sound.

Earning your beer
That photographers and artists should be drawn here for inspiration is understandable. There's so much to see and interpret, from the vistas, to the flora and fauna, and the human relationship with nature.

Kayakers and swimmers, depending on the tides, may find here sandy beaches and stoney shores, carved and beautified by nature. A short beach scramble or walk

from the pub brings you to Orlebar Point, a popular spot with divers drawn to its deep drop-off, sunken wrecks and abundant sea life. A short distance out rises the Orlebar Lighthouse on its rocky isle, a reminder that the sea can kill as much as please. A plaque pays tribute to a diver the sea took, a caution to others who would play within the temperamental bowels of the ocean.

It is easy to settle for a stroll along the unhurried roads, never at a loss for a view. On our visit, a heron shot past us, its long wings flapping gracefully, a flock of Canada geese squabbled upon the beach, the Duke Point Ferry glided past, and the clouds hung like rags on the distant Coast Mountains.

Like others of the Gulf Islands, these are wonderful places to visit in the off-season, when the world is quieter and less obstructed. Like the storm watch of the West Coast, the Isles have a winter allure you must experience to understand. And nowhere is this more apparent than while looking out a window at the Surf Pub.

SECTION FOUR Nanaimo

ESTABLISHMENT 45

The Crow and Gate Pub

2313 Yellow Point Road, Nanaimo, V9X 1W5
1-250-722-3731

Webpage – crowandgate.ca
Services – wi-fi, wheelchair-accessible with wheelchair-accessible washrooms

Location
On Yellow Point Road, off the northern junction with Cedar Road marked with signage. Set off the road near a large communications tower and marked with a sign.

What makes the Crow and Gate unique: setting, history, grounds and theme

The Crow and Gate holds the distinction of being the first neighbourhood pub in B.C. after the laws were altered in 1972 to make this possible. It has not rested on its laurels.
Modelled after pubs in England, whence came the first owner, Jack Nash, its half-timber (Tudor) interior decor with stucco, pegged wooden beams, imposing wood-burning hearths, seating to accommodate the few and the many (benches, booths and chairs and tables), heavy wood tables, authentic English paraphernalia (coasters, banners, stuffed fowl and such), wooden floors and carpeting all breathe Britannia. Despite its size, its configuration absorbs noise sufficiently to allow

for easy conversation, a fact enhanced by the absence of TVs. Its heartfelt warmth is no illusion on a blustery day.
The 10-acre property is highlighted by eye-catching gardens and manicured grounds. Tended lawns are interspersed with colourful

gardens so appealing they draw weddings and encourage patrons to enjoy the plentiful outdoor seating so as to drink in the atmosphere in the lap of Mother Nature.

Keen to support local and Island business, the family-owned and -operated pub carries five Island craft beers from three breweries: Phillips, Driftwood, and Hoyne (all from Victoria) as well as Merridale Cider from the Cowichan Valley. Those are complemented by a hearty presence of staples such as Smithwicks, Kilkenny, and Guinness on tap. Though keen to establish a reputation for a craft beer country pub atmosphere, the family-owned business has also worked diligently to garner a world-class reputation for its Scotch selection. It has been recognized by Whiskey Magazine as one of the best places in the world to savour the elixir. Twenty-five single malt Scotches are on the list.

The pub's unique name came about when Nash literally noticed a crow on a gate, though by happenstance, he originated from Sussex, where there is, in fact, a pub named Crow and Gate. A photo of that pub hangs beside the bar.

The Crow and Gate is very much a part of the Cedar community but is amenable to larger outside groups, such as bus tours.

Earning your beer
Numerous coastal parks and trails are nearby, including Hemer, Robertson, Blue Heron and the Cable Bay Trail. The latter trail has parking at the end of Nicola Road and provides for a two-kilometre hike to the wild water of Dodd Narrows, looking across to Mudge Island. From the trail end, a shoreline walk to the south brings you to Joan Point Park (nanaimo.ca/parks-search/parks/114-cable-bay-trail), Hazelwood Herb farm (hazelwoodherbfarm.com) joins McNab's corn maze (mcnabscornmaze.com), Yellow Point Cranberries (yellowpointcranberries.com) and Fredrich's Honey Farm (fredrichshoney.com) in affording rural offerings.

ESTABLISHMENT 46

The Wheatsheaf Pub

1866 Cedar Road, Nanaimo

        1-250-722-3141

Webpage -   wheatsheafpub.ca

Services–   wi-fi, wheelchair-accessible & wheelchair-accessible washrooms

Location
In Cedar on Cedar Road, across from the baseball park

What makes the Wheatsheaf Pub unique: history, architecture, community involvement and a hint of haunting

The "Wheaty," as it is affectionately known, has its feet deeply buried in the history of Cedar and remains a contemporary community focal point. Beginning public life as a stagecoach stop in 1882, it obtained an inn licence in 1885, courtesy of Queen Victoria, making it the oldest licensed inn in B.C. Original owner George Taylor died in 1904, and in 1910 the business was acquired by the Mahle family, who were followed in the mid-1970s by the Lingstroms. Art and Marion Hutt took over in 1978, and it remains in the family's hands today, now under the care of their three children.

Art and Marion also passed on a unique gift to the community of Cedar.

Across from the pub is the Wheatsheaf Sportsplex, owned and operated by the Hutts, composed of two large baseball diamonds. It's home to a variety of events in addition to sport, and includes a licensed concession stand and beer garden. Heavily involved in supporting local sports, the Wheatsheaf has received recognition from the B.C. Softball Hall of Fame.

Activities abound within the Wheaty's walls, where dart and cribbage leagues have long held court, and groups such as the Friday car club meet regularly. But these are not the original walls; those fell victim to fire in the 1920s and the architectural gem of today is an old house moved to the original site and adapted.

It is said the spirits of patrons past still hang around the place, their presence felt more than seen. Regulars who have passed on are remembered in photo and plaque in a corner niche—the same niche where early caretaker Danny Crocker breathed his last. There have been a few others whose final breaths were drawn within this space.

And the walls are alive with eye-catching mementoes. Stuffed animals and birds, historic sports photos, paintings and photos of the Wheaty over the years, historic baseball uniforms encased in glass, and the famed stuffed moose head. The head, brought in by Art and Marion, has become part of a local good-luck tradition. Newlyweds, birthday folk, intrigued tourists, and others hope for good luck by kissing its well-loved visage.

Much enlarged from its earliest days, the pub interior holds 102 patrons; the patio, encased in wrought-iron, 24 more. The patio is warmed by a fine gas fireplace framed in river rock. The 10 taps accommodate four craft beers, including the Island's own Phillips, Vancouver Island, and Hoyne brewery's products.

And food is not to be forgotten. The Wheatsheaf takes great pride in its menu, drawing attention to homemade pizzas, burgers and perogies.

There is also pride in how this longstanding business draws a large cross-section of the surrounding community, from young to old, and makes everyone welcome.

Earning your beer

Kitty-corner to the Wheatsheaf's liquor store is a new 150th birthday gift to Canada, marking a starting point for the 2.4-kilometre Morden Colliery walk to Hemer Provincial Park. The wide trail deposits the visitor alongside tranquil Holden Lake and provides access to Hemer Park's 11 kilometres of trails. The lower trail skirts the lake, while the upper pathway takes the visitor past a reedy pond with an open vista for bird watchers.

ESTABLISHMENT 47

The Cranberry Arms

1604 Cedar Road, Nanaimo
                                1-250-722-3112
Webpage –   cranberryarms.ca
Services–   wi-fi and wheelchair-accessible – men's
                                wheelchair-accessible wash room only

<u>Location</u>
On the edge of the community of Cedar, heading north to Nanaimo

<u>What makes the Cranberry Arms unique:</u> history

The clothes may be new, but the bones are old. "The Crannie," as it is affectionately known, has been around in one form or another since 1878, the creation of Michael and Anne Halloran, who won the property in 1875 in a card game.

Originally crowned the Cranberry Hotel, it fell into the hands of James, Michael Halloran's son, when Michael passed away at the tender age of 41. It would eventually take the name The Cranberry Arms.

It had many owners over the subsequent years, until Wendy Aldcroft took over in 1982 and turned the aging edifice into a popular neighbourhood pub. It passed into new hands in 2014.

Much remodelled from its pioneering days, it now sports a cafe as well as the pub, but the hotel is long closed. The pub's updated interior houses a singular reminder of of its history: an old photo showing the entranceway and top-floor balustrade, where there is now simply a wall. Bar and table seating accommodate 80 patrons in the bright interior, and the enclosed and partially covered patio a further 22.

The six taps offer two craft beers: Phillips of Victoria and Stanley Park of Vancouver. Pride is taken in home-cooked meals and 14 flavours of chicken wings served here. Licensing allows parents to bring in their little ones until 6 p.m.

Entertainment includes darts and pool, music trivia and karaoke nights, plus a live band every weekend.

The ghost of Michael Halloran might not recognize the place from the interior, but he would know the bones of his creation still stand after so many years.

Earning your beer
A five-kilometre drive from the Cranberry Arms is the trailhead for Jack Point and Biggs Park and a five-kilometre round-trip seaside hike that offers seaside vistas and forest. Be prepared for a few stairs and lots of twists and turns.

Turn right onto Cedar Road heading for Nanaimo, then right at the first stop sign. McMillan Road becomes Gordon Road, which you take until you reach an overpass over the Duke Point Road to the ferry. Take the overpass onto Maughan Road, and from there continue to Jackson Road, where you turn right and continue on to the end, where there is parking at the park trailhead. There is signage for Biggs Park along the way.

ESTABLISHMENT 48

The Dinghy Dock

Protection Island, Nanaimo
1-250-753-2373
Webpage – dinghydockpub.com
Services – limited wi-fi

Location
Floating in Nanaimo Harbour and moored to Protection Island. For non-boat people, there is an hourly Protection Island passenger ferry leaving from the inner harbour marina. Adult return fare is $9, and the 10-minute run across the busy harbour in the unique converted B.C. Ferries lifeboat is part of the experience.

What makes the Dinghy Dock unique: location, setting, and its distinction as the only registered floating pub in Canada.

This well-known Nanaimo feature has been part of the harbour landscape since it began as a Dinghy Dock establishment in 1989, with a dock where dinghies from moored boats could tie up and be shuttled in. Because it was classified as a marina, the facilities originally were required to include a shower, bakery and kitchen, and offered an indoor fishing hole for children. The fishing hole has moved outside for health reasons and the pub has grown into a formidable facility no longer requiring the appendages of a marina. Still, technically, this floating pub could be detached from the shore and motor off into the sunset.

Since 2004, the formerly seasonal business, now with new owners, has operated year-round.

The ferry fleet boats reminded me of the African Queen, for those old enough to remember Humphrey Bogart's tough little chugger daring jungle waterways. Safety is assured, as these former lifeboats, which carry a maximum 34 people across the sheltered waters of the harbour, are meant to carry up to 70 passengers in less-than-friendly waters during an emergency. For those with water wings, there are ample docking facilities with 200-feet moorage and an additional 50 feet at low tide, plus allowance for bobbing kayaks and canoes; exceptional accommodations have been provided for float planes, hovercraft and even an amphibious vehicle.

The pub interior, with its many windows, can literally bring the outside in when the garage door front is opened up to let patrons breathe in the sea air. Or you can chose to sit outdoors on the patio, to drink in the view of the busy harbour and the 180-degree-plus vista of mountains, water and islands. The nautical theme is reflected in marine memorabilia and rich, worn wood, complete with a band niche where various kinds of entertainment abound throughout the year. It is worth keeping an eye out for special package events; note also the pub's willingness to accommodate special groups.

The Dinghy Dock takes pride in involving itself in the community, including charitable activities, festivals (The Nanaimo Bite) and food-bank drives. This push for local connectedness extends to taps that tilt toward Vancouver Island businesses, including products of breweries Longwood of Nanaimo (such as the appropriately named Dock Side Lager), Phillips and Driftwood of Victoria, Red Arrow of Duncan, and a feature tap offering the latest up-and-coming local beer.

Pub events stretch throughout the year, with summer music fare leaning to rock 'n' roll and more laid-back strains otherwise owning the night. The first Saturday of every month features an open mic led by musician Brian Whitty, and there is a music trivia night on Thursday. Try sampling the bi-weekly acoustic nights, featuring local talent. Check the website for featured performers.

For many a year, on Wednesday nights from April to September, sailboat time trial races have been running from the pub, featuring up to 15 boats and sometimes even taking along a fortunate patron. And there is no better place to watch the twice-yearly fireworks that light the Nanaimo night harbour.

For locals, it is a place to boastfully take visitors, and for visitors who come to Nanaimo at any time of the year, not to experience the Dinghy Dock is akin to visiting Paris and missing the Eiffel Tower. Unique among the unique is the Dinghy Dock.

Earning your beer
Protection Island itself offers quiet walks down gravelled roads punctuated with beach access points opening out to views and vistas. The ramp to the island deposits you at the informal island parking lot awash with golf carts and access to a waterside park overseen by a blue heron rookery that in season is crowded with a reputed 25 nests. It is rumoured to have earned, in 2012, the title of second-largest such rookery in the world.

ESTABLISHMENT 49

The Lighthouse Bistro and Pub

50 Anchor Way Nanaimo V9R 7B5
                    1-250-754-3212
Webpage –   lighthousebistro.ca
Services-   wi-fi, wheelchair-accessible with wheel
                    chair-accessible washrooms

Location

Along the grand promenade in Nanaimo Harbour, near the parkade, sharing space with the Harbour Air departure lounge.

What makes the Lighthouse Pub and Bistro unique: architecture, location and setting

The first thing you notice here is the singular architecture so clearly associated with the pub/bistro name. A beacon rests atop the two-storey complex, hailing all to come savour its offerings of brew, food and vista, be it from the upstairs pub, the sheltered pub-like atmosphere of the detached outdoor patio cantilevered over the water, or the more sedate restaurant section, welcoming to both big and little folk. Standing like an island upon its pylons, embraced on all quarters by the sea, this architectural testament to the time-honoured lighthouse is as compelling externally as are the vistas of harbour and distant mountains that patrons can enjoy from inside or on the patio.

The pub/bistro began operations in 1987, after a competition was held to find a tenant for the unique architectural piece constructed by the harbour authority. Well maintained, it has lost none of its visual appeal and blends in with the world-class waterfront

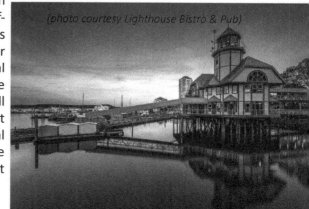

(photo courtesy Lighthouse Bistro & Pub)

complex that rims Nanaimo Harbour. The upstairs pub can be reached either directly along the upper-floor gangway or by stairs from the lower floor. The casual setting offers ample table and chair seating, ringed with windows that provide many-angled views of the expansive and busy harbour. For an unobstructed perspective, the outer deck provides a 180-degree vista.

In a tip to supporting Island industry, the Lighthouse's 12 combined taps (restaurant and pub) carry the products of Hoyne and Phillips breweries of Victoria, Longwood Brew Pub of Nanaimo, and Tugwell Creek Cider. A 20% discount on meals is applied for those flying Harbour Air.

There is much to see from the pub perch. The occasional great blue heron wings its graceful way amid boat and building. Fall brings out playful sea otters, float planes take turns owning the water and air, kayaks glide silently by, dragonboats ply the waters enlivened by their crews' chants, gulls squawk, and ferries make their ceaseless loops. Events—from the impressive Van Isle 360 (a circumnavigation of Vancouver Island by sailing vessels, some 60 in 2013), the Nanaimo Bathtub Race, dragonboat races, to harbour fireworks—provide unique entertainment. The fireworks in particular highlight the beauty of the harbour at night, aglitter with lights, and can be intimately viewed from the homey confines of the pub.

There is live music, with no cover charge, on Fridays and Saturdays, complemented by once-monthly Sunday jazz by award-winning performers, which does require paid admission.

In summer, the downstairs outdoor patio restaurant, sheltered from sun and rain, brings the outside in with a fun atmosphere. Pub-style warmth and relaxation with a barbecue theme and the embrace of sea air make it a popular seasonal draw.

A unique feature is the Lighthouse's crab sea-to-plate dinner. Patrons can watch their crab meal being plucked live from the underwater tank and have it cooked and on their plate within 20 minutes.

Like a beaconed island, the Lighthouse Pub is a vital part of the dynamic life of the Nanaimo Waterfront.

Earning your beer

There is more than enough at the harbour to keep a visitor active for more than two days while leaving the car parked in the sheltered parkade. Protection Island, Newcastle Island and Gabriola have their own specialized ferries, making just getting to them an adventure. Hiking and biking opportunities abound on the islands and along the long promenade, which passes through child-welcoming Maffeo Sutton Park and far beyond. Nearby is the historic Bastion museum, and dotting the promenade are historic photos of old Nanaimo, with intriguing tales and vistas. The music of buskers fills the air, and the walkway is alive with people. You do not want to miss the harbour if fortune favours you with a visit to Nanaimo.

ESTABLISHMENT 50

White Sails Brewery & Taproom

125 Comox Road, Nanaimo

	1-250-754-2337
Webpage –	whitesailsbrewing.com
Services –	wi-fi, wheelchair-accessible with wheel chair-accessible washrooms

Location
Near the corner of Comox and Terminal Avenue, across the road from parking at Maffeo Sutton Park

What makes the White Sails unique: history, and it's a brewery
When the famed phoenix burned and was reborn, no one said it needed to be reborn exactly the same. The White Sails pub rests on the ashes of the old Newcastle Hotel, but a different wind fills its sails.

The Newcastle Hotel was built in the late 1800s by the owner of one of the Pacific Northwest's largest breweries: Union Brewing. After many years, it succumbed to fire and was replaced by a new, purpose-built pub known as the Foundry. In 2015 it reopened under new ownership and a new philosophy, as White Sails Brewing.
Focussing on beer-making and a belief in collaborating with the community, the new endeavour has embraced collaboration with other community businesses and groups.

Lacking its own kitchen and devoting attention to beer-making, White Sails has established working relationships with food suppliers, distilleries and wineries. It recycles brewing waste with a local farmer, and it offers a "guest tap" for other brewers' craft beers. For the community, it offers space for a poetry group, artists group, musicians, and a Sunday yoga group enjoying "mindful" beer tasting. It's also family-friendly. To this, add music coupled with "cask" night. The absence of TVs and presence of board games emphasize the pub's community-building vision. The works of well-known local artist Grant Leier adorn the walls.

All of this is done in a spacious environment centred around a huge gas fireplace framed in brick, and under a soaring roof. An assortment of seating options, ranging from communal tables, bar stools and small tables to cushioned seats and sofas, is spread throughout the large, open space, which is augmented by niches and a summer patio. Large windows flood the environment with natural light. At the back, you can view the workings of the brewing process.

Products made here feature local names such as Shack Island Stout, Old City Smash, Departure Bay Session Ale, Yellow Point Pale ale, the international award-winning Mount Benson IPA and Snake Island CDA, and more—all of which pour forth from the pub's 16 taps.
Parking is available behind the pub and across the street at Maffeo Sutton Park. A bus stop is conveniently located across the road.
It is a fair wind that fills the sails of this pub.

Earning your beer
Maffeo Sutton park is home to the annual Blues Festival and the Nanaimo Marine Festival, featuring the International Bathtub Races. From the park's dock you can catch the summer ferry to forested Newcastle Island and spend much of the day wandering its trails and enjoying its sights.

ESTABLISHMENT 51

The Coach & Horses

321 Selby Street, Nanaimo
1-250-591-9450
Webpage – coachandhorsesbc.ca
Services – wi-fi, wheelchair-accessible with wheelchair-accessible washrooms

Location
The Esquimalt & Nanaimo Railway Station in the old section of Nanaimo, near Selby and Fitzwilliam.

What makes The Coach & Horses unique: history, architecture, theme and range of brew offerings

None other than the famous imbiber and first prime minister of Canada, Sir John A. MacDonald, was there to open the original E&N Station on July 25, 1886. Some 126 years later, on July 25, 2013, the latest incarnation opened, with the station rising phoenix-like from the ashes of a 2007 arson blaze. The restoration was a community effort the brought the station back as closely as possible to its original state, using, where possible, original materials. And there was a new addition that might have pleased the first PM to no end: Fibber Magee's Irish Pub, which became the Nanaimo Taphouse Restaurant followed by the current Coach & Horses.

Should he arrive by rail nowadays, MacDonald would have to stride only seven steps from train to patio to partake of the elixirs of the gods. Freight trains still rumble by, lending their song and rattle to the refurbished station for the patrons' nostalgic entertainment, while many an Islander hopes for the return of passenger service from Courtenay to Victoria, with a spur line to West Coast waters at Port Alberni.

When that day arrives, the ticket station will share space with the expansive pub and its warm, red interior, which offers seating alternatives ranging from cozy couples to joyous groups. Benches, booths, bar seating and tables even allow the option of bringing children along. The long character bar is strewn with colour and the pump trappings of a well-equipped establishment.

Upstairs, where railway employees once made use of dorms and other facilities, are equally rich settings for groups, including a separate bar-served section replete with a niche for entertaining, and another section warmed by a hearth. Windows let patrons gaze out over the tracks, with their humming history of over 120 years. Up and down, there is no mistaking the care, attention and commitment that has gone into the Coach & Horses.

For brew aficionados, 16 taps dispense a range of British, German, and Island craft beers, plus draft Guinness. The taps rotate, save for the Guinness, but Island craft beers Phillips and Nanaimo's own Longwoods are regulars.

The Coach & Horses also has a patio trackside, with a full view of passing trains, lying in wait for the day when that reborn passenger train comes cruising to a halt nearby—an image to put a smile on Sir John A.'s face.

Earning your beer
The Coach & Horses is a short walk from all that downtown Nanaimo and its harbour have to offer, but there is much to experience even in the immediate area. The neighbourhood is alive with unique, colourful and funky shops that are part of the emerging reinvention of the city's old town. Spend the day exploring shops and market centres or wandering the old neighbourhoods, residential and commercial. With the hoped-for return of passenger service putting both Victoria and Courtenay within easy train commute, this is the heart of a new Nanaimo vibrancy. Check out the walking tour at oldcityquarter.com.

ESTABLISHMENT 52

The Longwood Brew Pub

5775 Turner Road, Nanaimo, V9T 6L8
1-250-729-8225
Webpage –   longwoodbrewpub.com
Services –   wi-fi, wheelchair-accessible with
wheelchair-accessible washrooms

Location
In Longwood Station Plaza on on Highway 19A (Island Highway North) between North Town Shopping Centre (formerly Rutherford Mall) and Woodgrove Centre.

What makes the Longwood Brew Pub unique: architecture, and it's a brew pub.

Walking into the Longwood restaurant/pub complex is rather like walking into a welcoming mansion. Entering through ornate etched-glass doors, you are greeted by dark wood paneling, high ceilings and wrought-iron railings that continue down the open stairwell to the informal yet classy pub.
To your left, open glass reveals the working body of the brew process. A comfortable leather couch awaits when you need to wait for a table. A world of special woods unfurls in the bar, walls (American dark cherry) and floors (Jatoba), broken by a large rock-framed fireplace that serves as the central focus. Above the fireplace, a historical Nanaimo photo recalls the early, heady days of brewing in the coal city, as do a number of smaller photos dotting the hallway walls. Multi-paned windows are all about, and on the opposite side of the hearth sprawls a well-lit pool room with a nine-foot table. Longwood is part of a pool league circuit involv-

ing 10 teams and five venues. That the table is free and not coin-operated is a draw. Outside is a patio enclosed in lattice that accommodates groups and summer barbecues. Table-and-chair seating is accompanied by bar seating. The buzz of conversation is enhanced by low background music and strategically placed, high-definition TVs set to sports stations.

For special events, the third floor offers the equally rich setting of the Brewery Room, which can accommodate 42 standing and 30 seated. The Longwood is surrounded by well-tended landscaping, from which it seems to emerge in oneness. A smiling Buddha would not look out of place. Since May 2000, the brew pub has been making a name for itself for both brew and pub. To accommodate demand, it has opened a separate brewery while continuing its in-house brewing. Tours of the brewing facility and operation can be arranged on request.

There are 105 recognized styles of beer in the world, and the Longwood has access to 40 recipes, maintaining nine taps in operation at any time. Eight carry the regular brewed fare, while the ninth carries a seasonal offering. These include cold ales Longwood (5% alcohol), Czech Pilsener (5.1%), India Pale (6.5%), Dunkelweizenbrau (wheat beer at 5.1%), Framboise (raspberry-flavoured, at 5%) and cellar beers drawn on "English machines" (being pumped, as the beer is non-carbonated): Extra Special Bitters (5.5%), Irish Red Ale and Russian Imperial Stout (7.5%). These are complemented by a guest tap: Merridale Cider, from the Cowichan Valley.

For true beer aficionados, the website goes into the details of brewing, and a tour is there for the asking. To the beer list are added ample options of wine and liquor. If you want to try a few beers side by each you can purchase a sampler of four brews in six-ounce glasses—a great way to note the taste differences. And the tour history will be courtesy of brew master Graham Payne. The pub's commitment to purity is certified by its membership in CAMRA (Campaign for Real Ale).

As new as the pub is, a poignant connection with its past stands old and proud outside its doors. The shopping centre and pub were built on farmland, and when the last member of the pioneer family who actually worked the land passed away, his son held a celebration-

of-life ceremony at the pub. There, amid the photos of remembrance, was one of the farmhouse with a tall tree beside it. Through all the construction and years that have passed, the tree remains, now rising more than 50 feet. Ask where to look for it when you pass the doors.

Family-friendly, the Longwood's main-floor restaurant has gained a reputation for fine, fresh cuisine enhanced by locally produced ingredients. Great pride is taken in offering exceptional fare in refined surroundings, at a reasonable price.

Earning your beer
Nearby, in the midst of the city, stretches Long Lake, offering swimming, boating, fishing, picnicking, sunbathing and washrooms. Close by runs the E&N rail line, with its ever-expanding multi-purpose side trail destined to the run the length of the city. Fifteen minutes by car will have you savouring the oceanside at city parks like Neck Point and Piper's Lagoon, with rambling trails and seaside mountain vistas.

ESTABLISHMENT 53

The Black Bear Pub

6201 Dumont Road, Nanaimo
1-250-390-4800
Webpage – blackbearpub.com
Services – wi-fi, wheelchair-accessible with wheelchair-accessible washrooms

Location
Take Metral Road to Doumont Road and head inland. It will be on your left just after passing under the Highway #1 overpass. Ample parking on site.

What makes the Black Bear unique: theme, setting and view

The Black Bear began life in 1976 as Quigley's Harp and Shamrock, reflecting the Welsh and Irish backgrounds of its initial owners. In 1989, John Wicks, himself a transplanted Londoner, took it over and maintained its British theme, which has been continued by the present management.

The Black Bear prides itself on its food as well as beverages, along with an atmosphere of neighbourly comfort; it's a place where groups of one to many can gather to socialize in a safe and welcoming environment.

The pub name came from a story related to John by a local farmer when he was mulling over new names. Seems the farmer had been out working his fields and was rather preoccupied when, all of a sudden, he looked up to find the biggest black bear he had ever seen approaching him. He screamed; the bear (in his own way) did

likewise; and the two sped off in opposite directions. And now the bear is immortalized in name and image.

Upon the walls and spread about the pub are an assortment of bear items and paraphernalia, with one item in particular standing out: a bear holding a beer. The half-timbered, stuccoed walls are adorned with memorabilia ranging from horse brasses to copper pots to collector plates, knickknacks and such, all lending themselves to the cozy British theme. Fittingly, the feature burger is the Big Bear Burger.

The big feature of the pub, both physically and psychologically, is the expansive outer deck and the ever-changing vista of parkland, lake and mountain. Set on 2.6 acres, the deck and lawns leave the impression that you are on a private estate. The moods of season and day are always playing with the view, sometimes robbing patrons of their view of Mount De Cosmos (named after B.C.'s first premier, Amour de Cosmos—Lover of the Universe—whose real name was Bill Smith) and Mount Benton, while at other times throwing the whole panorama into glorious sight.

Despite being close to the highway and greater Nanaimo, there is a sense here of being away from it all as you sit, beer in hand, watching the sun play upon the mountains and lake. Like a pub of the Isles sitting on the edge of tranquility.

Earning your beer
Hiking and biking groups make use of the trails in the forests beyond the Black Bear; one leads to Ammonite Falls (nanaimoinformation.com/ammonite-falls.php), where fossil remains are to be found.

ESTABLISHMENT 54

Lantzville Pub

7197 Lantzville Road, Lantzville
1-250-390-4019
Webpage – lantzvillepub.ca
Services – wi-fi, wheelchair-accessible with wheel chair-accessible washrooms

Location
Take Ware Road off the Trans Canada Highway and head toward the ocean. At the end of the road, turn left and you will spot it almost immediately on your left.

What makes the Lantzville Hotel/Pub unique: history, setting and view

Some say Lantzville survived because the Lantzville Hotel survived, when all around it appeared evidence of decline: mine closures, the Depression and the re-routing of the highway. That theory seems less of a stretch when you see the space it occupies and learn a little about the place and the people who participated in its rich history.

The modern pub owns 11 taps, of which two are rotating, carrying IPAs and local island craft products. These have included the products of Phillips (Victoria), Riot (Chemainus), Mr. Arrowsmith (Ladysmith) and Wolf (Nanaimo), to name a few. In a nod to today's greater social responsibility, a reduced-cost taxi service is available.

Despite the modern trappings of mounted televisions, the high ceilings, wooden half-walls, front veranda and tall storefront windows, opening to an ocean and mountain view, lodge it firmly in its historical roots. The window vista speaks volumes about the pub's evolution and the place it holds in this small community of 3,000. A spe-

cial character element is the dark wood, antique bar originally hailing from Missoula, Montana, reputedly from a saloon once frequented by outlaw Jesse James. A century old when it was purchased in 1975, the bar's historical richness has only grown with all that has transpired here since it arrived at the Lantzville. A polite inquiry may get you the chance to see the filled-in gunshot holes.

The story goes back to 1925, when Rosa Caillett, a recent immigrant from France, and her son, Abel, set up shop with their newly built hotel in the mining town of Lantzville. She and Abel had had an adventurous and meandering trip through the Canadian West before they set down roots on the coast. They soon had a liquor licence and began carving out a diversified business that included a gas station, telephone service, and restaurant to complement their 10-room hotel, with additional dorm facilities up top. The luxuries of electricity, running water and indoor plumbing were slowly added, and the little business along the main Vancouver Island road eked out an existence. Homegrown fruits and vegetables, plus their own farm-raised chicken reflected the resourcefulness of Rosa and Abel. In time, they took over management of the old miners' homes that had been part of the Lantzville Coal Mine before it faded from history.

Rosa never did remarry, her husband having died before she reached the coast, but she was reputed to have maintained a significant other, one Jim Tweedhope, who did his bit in helping the establishment survive. In 1932, she passed away in the hotel, and it is suspected it is her ghost who haunts the hallways of the storied building. Historic photos adorning the walls include one of Rosa's stern visage, still overseeing what she created. Another occasional apparition, a man in a jacket standing by the bar, is thought to be Jim Tweedhope. A year before Rosa's death, her grandson, Armand Caillet, who was to eventually own and operate the hotel, was born inside it. The hotel would finally pass from Caillet family hands on Oct. 5, 1981.

An excellent book written by Armand recounts the family's history with the hotel from its inception to its sale, and in the process reveals much of the early life of Lantzville and Vancouver Island. It can be purchased at the pub.

This venerable old pub continues to be a vital part of of its small community, with little suggestion of decline. Just ask the ghosts.

Earning your beer

Nestled in the heart of Lantzville, the pub is a short trek from the sea for enjoying the vista or taking a stroll, with a number of beach access points at the ends of nearby streets. Kayakers sometimes put in at the beach and trundle up to the pub for liquid respite, and folk commonly take up chairs by the beach in the evening to drink in the declining sun reflecting upon ocean and mountain. Visitors can catch the Sunday farmers market in season, hike or bike the nearby parkway trail, or put in some rounds at the Winchelsea Golf Course. An ideal way to end the day is to spend time with a fine brew and a great sunset view by the pub's front windows.

SECTION FIVE Mid-North Island

ESTABLISHMENT 55

The Rocking Horse Pub

2038 Sanders Road, Nanoose Bay
                    1-250-468-1735
Webpage –   rockinghorsepub.ca
Services –   wi-fi, wheelchair-accessible with wheel
                    chair-accessible washrooms

Location
Well signposted off of North West Bay Road, running between Parksville and Nanoose Bay.

What makes the Rocking Horse unique: setting, theme, decor

An old song, "Cowboy Jock from Skye," sung by famed Scottish crooner Andy Stewart, immediately came to mind when I learned how this western Canadian cowboy setting became melded with Celtic roots.
Leaving the highway behind and travelling along the winding gravel drive, you are met by horses and an impression of space and casual hospitality. Ample parking, a neighbouring stable, horses in their paddock, and a forested horizon create an unhurried atmosphere. That we were greeted happily at the door by a tiny Jack Russell terrier only added to that feeling.

It is not surprising this place feels homey; the Rocking Horse was built as a private residence in 1972 for Arthur and Ada Knight and converted to a pub in 1977. After going through numerous owners, additions and renovations, it landed in the hands of present owners David and Karen Willoughby in 2004. The property occupies five acres, with a workshop, barn and the British-themed pub, with a pas-

toral outdoor patio granting a view of guests to some curious neighbours: a laid-back troop of alpacas and llamas. The animals casually survey the outdoor imbibers with a chewing curiosity of seemingly great philosophical depth. Gardens add to the welcoming atmosphere.

A herd of wild horses, in a frozen painted moment, greet you at the entrance. You face the choice of going left to the more sedate dining area, with sectional privacy, or right, to the grandly group-friendly pub section. The entirety of the building is given over to the pub, with your choice of atmosphere, and the whole place accommodates 138 bottoms. Seating ranges from bar to booth to tables and benches. The group-friendly section houses a big-screen TV, worn wood floors to accommodate dancing, wainscotted walls, a rock hearth, and a wealth of windows for daylight brightness. Spacious and welcoming, it is a setting for Celtic frivolity. Jock would enjoy the annual January Robbie Burns Night, complete with haggis, piper and Scottish menu. March brings on Celtic Chaos to celebrate St. Patrick's Day, complete with its own Irish menu. For a further touch of the Isles, one of the 13 taps offers Guinness. Many years of housing a New Year's party with the same blues band suggests the place is both popular and consistent.

The more sedate dining area offers a cottage-style setting with carpeting, a hearth, more privacy, memorabilia adorning the walls of wood and stucco, and French doors leading out to the quiet gardens.
You can enjoy garden solitude and pastoral space amid the chirping of birds and the glassy-eyed gaze of llamas.

A popular year-round destination, the Rocking Horse has its regular groups, such as a local walking club, Red Hat Society, and newcomers' clubs. With its three distinct sections, it offers a wide range of atmospheres with something for virtually everyone.

A welcoming British pub set amid gardens, neighbouring horses and their ilk is certainly enough to get Cowboy Jock off his steed to doff his boots and slake his thirst.

<u>Earning your beer</u>
The expanse of Rathtrevor Provincial Park is within a few minutes' drive, with its seemingly endless seaside sands and mountain vistas, as are the broad, sandy beaches of Parksville, both with ample parking.

ESTABLISHMENT **56**

The Black Goose Inn

Ocean Beach Acres Resort, Parksville
1-250-586-1001
Webpage – blackgooseinn.com
Services – wi-fi, wheelchair-accessible, wheelchair-accessible washrooms

Location
The Inn sign, a black goose with bagpipes, greets you at the entry to Beach Acres Resort (off of Resort Drive, south of Parksville), and you will find both the Inn and ample parking just before the road dips down to the ocean.

What makes the Black Goose Inn unique: architecture, location, setting, hauntings, history and theme

Samuel Maclure was a self-taught architect, reputedly the first non-native child born in New Westminster when his first cries were heard in 1860. His talents were most strongly imprinted on Vancouver and Victoria, but here, with a majestic ocean view facing the Sechelt Peninsula, long, sandy beaches, and the snow-tipped Coast Mountain range, he left a mark as vibrant today as when it was first constructed in 1921, just south of Parksville. And, today, it is far more accessible.

The Black Goose came to life as a private residence, and not inexpensively for the Beattie family. MacLure-designed homes were so demanding that contractors added a surcharge to their contracts. Constructed in the manner of a Scottish hunting lodge, its board-and-batten design, with shingle siding, a shingled roof and brick enhancements, looks

as formidable today as when it was constructed. While still a private home, it was visited by celebrities such as Rudyard Kipling and actress Faye Rae, and its opulence has faded only a little. You can view photos of the original family owners and guests in the foyer. It was an era!

As that era faded, the home eventually took on a new life as a restaurant and came into the hands of the Ivens family, who reopened it in December 2010 as the Black Goose. It is joined by their other unique pub, the Fox and Hounds in Ladysmith.

The interior great room greets you with a large, crackling, wood-burning fireplace whose mantel bears a model of the famed Cutty Sark set against embossed woodwork and wood panelling. Above hangs a wrought-iron chandelier, and close by is an ornately embellished 1865 piano, upon which rests a modern black goose statuette. The open-beam ceiling rises high to its peak and the entirety is horseshoed by the second floor gallery, which offers a full view of all who enter the great room. Two antechambers greet the eye with rich reddish-tinted walls and white trim, providing an aura of intimacy.

The Snug, complete with wood-burning fireplace, houses the pub bar, where both food and drink are ordered. There's a strong British theme in both fare and beverages. Inside, bar seating and table-and-chair options can accommodate up to 60 patrons, all enjoying personal space. Views from the leaded-glass windows are of surrounding trees and cottages or the grand ocean vista, preceded by the Inn's gardens and lawn, where outside picnic-table seating is available.

This is a place that feels welcoming to one and all, giving regular folk an idea of what it must have been like for the affluent residents of years gone by. Refined and classic as the building may be. there is nothing stuffy about it. Notably, as it's a pub-style restaurant, children are allowed. Welcoming, for sure. Why else would one, perhaps two, ghosts insist on hanging around? Andrew, the basement ghost, being a bit of a prankster, is given to moving items and leaving doors open, while there are suspicions a second ghost, female, occupies the upper floor.

The 16 taps run strong to brews from the British Isles, including draft Guinness, but they also carry products of Longwood (Nanaimo), Phillips (Victoria), Riot Brewery (Chemainus) and Merridale Cider (Cowichan Valley). Maclure finished 450 commissions in his illustrious career; no doubt he would be pleased to tip a fine pint of Vancouver Island craft beer at the Black Goose and bask in the glow of his legacy. Perhaps Andrew would join him with a pint of pale ale.

Earning your beer

You can walk down to the beach from the Black Goose and stroll north or south; north takes you to Rathtrevor Beach Provincial Park. The vast expanse of these famed beaches at low tide attracts walkers in the hundreds while still leaving space for everyone, including squawking water fowl. Free public parking is available in the park.

You are a short distance from Parksville, with its broad intertidal beaches, community park and waterfront walkway. July and August features the renowned sandcastle competitions (parksvillebeachfest.ca).

ESTABLISHMENT 5 7

The Shady Rest Pub

3109 West Island Highway, Qualicum Beach, V9K 2C5
1-250-752-9111
Webpage –   shadyrest.ca
Services –   wi-fi, wheelchair-accessible with wheel
chair-accessible washrooms

Location
Water side of the highway, along the wide expanse of Qualicum Beach.
Ample parking.

What makes the Shady Rest unique: location, setting, view, history

It was a quieter world in 1924, when Thomas Kinkade first built the
Shady Rest Hotel along the scenic shoreline of Qualicum Beach. Much
has changed since those days, but not the breadth of the beach, the
stunning maritime view, nor the presence of the Shady. Over its history,
it has embraced fishing charters, gas pumps, bus stops, rental waterfront
cabins and a hotel, but there has always been a pub. Today it stands accompanied by its adjacent restaurant.
The Kinkades kept the business in the family until 1985, when it was
sold to Wayne Duncan, a former part-owner of the historic Prairie Inn
in Saanichton. Under his guidance, both the pub and restaurant have
vastly expanded.

(photo courtesy Shady Rest Pub)

The pub interior is com-
fortable and unassuming,
with ample space and
seating to accommodate
groups in numbers large
and small. A gas fireplace
holds the focus in one
area, while two others
offer an inner sanctum
and a window-framed
niche. Integral to the at-

mosphere is the full-length window walls, which bathe the interior with natural light and open up an eye-popping panoramic vista.

The 180-degree-plus view encompasses the sprawl of the beach and beyond to mountain, sea and islands: Lasqueti Island, dwarfed by Texada and the looming snow-capped Coast Range. The outer deck, in season, opens up a totally unobstructed, wind-washed vista. Nor is the pub's view a static one: there are passing cruise ships, water craft of all sorts, kayaks, beach walkers and, in season, herring-drawn sea lions, otters, seals, flurries of nagging gulls, and the fishing fleet. To this, add the ever-changing moods of season and hour, and your gaze can be long captivated.

Popular with locals and tourists alike, the long beach walkway and wide tidal flats allow for thirst-inducing and stomach-rumbling exercise, for which the Shady Rest oasis provides quick relief. Here you can enjoy a journey replete with nature's entertainment and beachside services.

Long a part of the community and the Island culture, the Shady dedicates many of its 11 taps to Island craft beers. Regularly available are the products of the Driftwood, Phillips and Hoyne Breweries of Victoria, joined on a rotating basis by those of Mount Arrowsmith Brewing (Parksville), Gladstone Brewing (Courtenay), Riot Brewing (Chemainus), and Red Arrow Brewing (Duncan), to name a few. The only way to know for sure what's on tap on a given day is to ask your server. Just as striking is the Shady's commitment to local producers, as reflected in its menus. Suppliers and their distance from the Shady are identified, along with icons to signal vegetarian and gluten-free fare.
Live entertainment owns the floor on Saturday, with dance music provided by local talent.

The Shady has set deep roots here with its continuous operation, strong community ownership and sincere efforts to support local and island businesses.

Earning your beer
The tended, wheelchair-accommodating beach walkway is long enough to work up a decent thirst and appetite, regardless of where you park your chariot. There is much to draw and hold your attention here and thereby add time to your jaunt. For birders, there is the added benefit

of a range of waterfowl and the Brant goose-viewing platform, which draws hardy avian fans out in season.

As if this weren't enough, there are also festivals attracting folk to town and beach. Beach Fest, in July, has been running for a few years, with games and music events. The Father's Day Show and Shine brings over 575 show cars to town, and upwards of 30,000 people (seasidecruizers. com). Twenty years and counting, Fire and Ice sees downtown Qualicum given over to pedestrians, with local eateries, including the Shady, competing for honours, along with a chili contest (fire) and ice sculpting (ice). Birders gather for the Brant Festival, which runs March to April (brant-festival.bc.ca). The local tourism office is conveniently located along the beach walkway and is the source of much advice on things to see and do. It dispenses material on local bird walks, Little Qualicum Falls Provincial Park, and Horne Lake Caves, and maps of both Parksville and Qualicum.

ESTABLISHMENT 58

Crown and Anchor Roadhouse

6120 West Island Highway, Qualicum Bay
1-250-757-9444
Webpage – crownandanchor.ca
Services – wi-fi

Location

On old Vancouver Island Highway (Oceanside Route) at Qualicum Bay, made conspicuous by the bright "Road House" sign. Within hailing distance of the bay where the Parksville Qualicum Journal proclaimed, in 1951, that a sea monster had frolicked about in full view of a host of witnesses for a couple of hours, never to be seen again.

What makes the Crown and Anchor unique: ghosts, history, location

Some claim that walls hold memories of events that transpire within them. If so, the Crown and Anchor speaks when circumstances serve its purpose.

These walls reputedly first rose as part of the Forest Inn resort in the 1920s (though there are references to the site being the home of a girls' school as early as 1904), the creation of one Joe Charlebois. In the '30s the inn passed to the Newman family (who changed the name to Casa del Mar), and then the State family in the '40s and '50s. It served as a resort and residence before, in 1970, becoming a pub. Holly, who worked as a server at the Crown in years past, now shares ownership with partner Jerry.

Easily accessible, with ample parking fore and aft, the wood/brick exterior has the feel of a roadside inn of the horse-and-wagon days—a welcome

sight on a long day's journey. Its three spacious rooms are enhanced by a pool table room and an enclosed outer patio with shaded table and chairs. Decorated in rich woods with brick accenting, stucco, and panelled walls, it has a cozy atmosphere made more so by an ornate bar topped with heritage stained glass, inset with carvings from a door taken from Hy's Mansion in Vancouver, and a welcoming wood-burning stove with a brick hearth.

Perhaps these comfortable surroundings have induced certain otherworldly spirits, allegedly witnessed by both staff and customer, to stay. Stories recount coffee filters comically flying off horizontally and people being poked in the ribs, but also the somber sight of a little girl on the steps—perhaps relating to the era of the girls' school? Bar, table and bench seating ensures spots for singles, couples and groups, all offering bright lighting and views of the outdoors. There are country jam sessions every Sunday, an open mic on Wednesday, and bluegrass on Thursday nights.

Historic photos line the walls. This is a spot with the atmosphere of a community gathering place. And the walls watch and listen, perhaps embracing stories of the present to be recounted to a later audience. Or maybe a little girl, forever young, is playing on the stairs, knowing more than we can even guess.

Earning your beer
You can easily while away a day or so in the environs of Qualicum Bay. Parks at Spider Lake and Horne Lake, with their hiking, boating, swimming and biking options, complement unique nearby features such as the fish hatchery, the "goats-on-roof" market at Coombs (a 20-minute drive) and the yawning mouths of the Horne Lakes Caves. Arrowsmith Golf Course, with its inviting, verdant green, is a short haul away. You could even try fishing for sea serpent in the bay.
Not far back, along the private road through a campground, run the E&N train tracks. The promised return of rail is coupled with long-term plans to run a hiking/biking/horse trail alongside the tracks. When that becomes a reality, the Crown and Anchor could prove a refreshing highlight to a healthy jaunt.

ESTABLISHMENT 59

Twin City Brewing

4503 Margaret Street, Port Alberni
                          1-778-419-2739
Webpage –   twincitybrewing.ca
Services –   wi-fi, wheelchair-accessible with wheel
                          chair-accessible washrooms

Location
At the corner of Margaret Street and Southgate Road

What makes Twin City Brewery unique: brews its own beer,
family-friendly

Twin City's name harks back to the fact Port Alberni was once the twin
communities of Port Alberni and Alberni. Its authenticity is reflected in
its logo and the people behind it.

Twin City Brewing Company was born out of long-time Port Alberni
resident Aaron Colyn's desire to create a hub for local folk to gather,
and to combine his background in the sciences with his passion for the
art of craft beer making. This pub is the new kid on the block, having
opened in March 2017.

The building began life as a government liquor store in 1946, a photo
of which hangs beside the bar in a place of honour, before spending 40
years as a printing shop.
Its story came full circle
when Twin City Brewing
Company took over, with
the crossed-axe logo,
representing the town's
lumber history, replacing
the government logo.

The interior atmosphere
is one perhaps best de-

scribed as Port Alberni chic, suggesting that what appears rough-hewn can nonetheless reveal polish. Walls, tables and lighting all incorporate "repurposed" materials: lights from a lumber warehouse, sheet metal from an old barn. There is communal seating at large tables, meant to encourage strangers to interact, smaller tables for more intimacy, stools at the bar, and window ledges. Thanks to its high ceilings and many windows, the pub is awash with natural light, creating a feeling of space and comfortable informality.

Running eight taps, the pub offers four regular beers, one or two seasonals, and one to two rotating guest taps. The day of our visit, products of Phillips (Victoria) and Cumberland Brewing Company were guest taps; also on stream was Twin City Sparkling Leotard, a grapefruit Radler with a minuscule 2.5% alcohol content, for those conscious of their alcohol intake. For those who like to sample, there are beer flights allowing for comparative tastings.

Keeping their focus local, the brewery doesn't bottle, can, or distribute its beer. Those wanting to sample their product must come to them.

And if you need further enticement, the pub prides itself on offering a different special pizza every week.

Plans are to add an outdoor patio, reached via a raised garage door, which will give dog lovers an opportunity to let their dogs sit beside them outside the railing.

Port Alberni chic is alive and well, proving you can be both authentic and serve a polished product.

Earning your beer
Stopping in at the splendid Visitor Information Centre on your way into town can net you a trail map detailing 13 different trails to explore. Of those, seven are located in town, the longest being the Rogers Creek Nature Trail, a moderate eight-kilometre circuit. It connects with two other, more challenging, trails that add a further 4.5 kilometres. There is ample opportunity for hiking without straying far afield from the oasis that is Twin City Brewery.

ESTABLISHMENT 60

The Fanny Bay Inn

7480 Island Highway, Fanny Bay
1-250-335-2323
Webpage – fannybayinn.com
Services – wi-fi, wheelchair-accessible with wheel chair-accessible washrooms

Location
Some 22 kilometres north of Qualicum Beach on the old Island Highway; heading north, look for the road sign on the right, once you pass Fanny Bay Trading Company on your left.

What makes the Fanny Bay Inn unique: start with the name, but add history, oysters and location; plenty of parking space.

This much-modified roadhouse, known locally as the FBI, has been guarding bay and road since 1938, when its clientele largely consisted of loggers and sawmill workers and its comforts did not yet include electricity. Its well-tended exterior belies its many hard years. It's now a respectable, lodge-like, two-storey structure topped with roofing tile, with painted shake siding and stucco, and faced with river rock.

The interior is equally modernized, except for the brick-faced hearth and true wood-burning fireplace — one of the few so remaining fireplaces seen in my pub journeys. The flames warm a cozy area running to the side and in front of the bar to a niche overlooking a long stretch of lawn with a view on the horizon of Bayne's Sound and Denman Island. Bright and welcoming seating ranges from table to bench and stool, providing space for single patrons, couples and

groups. The expanse of lawn has picnic-table seating and in the summer is home to music and barbecues, with its ocean vista setting.

Of special note are the oysters served here. You see, Fanny Bay is not your regular bay. It is said to be home to the finest oysters harvested anywhere in North America. Local producer and neighbour Fanny Bay Oysters is the supplier supporting this unique and local menu feature. The company's products can be purchased at the Fanny Bay Oyster Shop, located at Buckley Bay (terminal for the ferry to Denman and Hornby Islands), just north of the FBI. Check fannybayoysters.com for details.

Sunday music jams begin at 5 p.m. and are regularly hosted by the Ryder Bachman Band. Vancouver Island craft beers on tap are represented by the Vancouver Island Brewery (Victoria), Gladstone Brewing Company (Courtenay), and the Cumberland Brewing Company.

Long a part of the community, the FBI sponsors fundraisers such as the penny drive, in which a wheelbarrow gets pushed all the way to Courtenay while being filled with pennies along the way, as well as the motorcycle toy run to Port Alberni.

Conveniently, the last bus to Courtenay and Parksville leaves at 10 p.m., offering a nice alternative for those looking for transportation options. One can only wonder if J. Edgar Hoover ever came north to check out the oysters and the federal bureau's namesake.

Earning your beer

To the south about one kilometre is the four-kilometre Wacky Woods trail, filled with the artistic endeavours of one George Sawchuk, who passed away in early 2012. From his arrival on the scene in 1974 to his demise, he employed unique forms of artistic expression to reflect his various perceptions of man's relationship with nature. A Google search will bring up a host of photos and descriptions of what is a one-of-a-kind stroll that is perhaps fated to oblivion, given the loss of its creator.

Look for Ship Point Road, across the road from the Fanny Bay Community Centre, and take it to "Little Way," turn left and then left again on Bates Drive. Continue to the dead-end and look for the unmarked trail.

ESTABLISHMENT 61

Thatch Pub and Restaurant

4305 Shingle Spit Road, Hornby Island
1-250-335-0136
Webpage –   thatchpub.ca
Services–   wi-fi, wheelchair-accessible with wheel
                  chair-accessible washrooms

Location
Kitty-corner to the BC Ferries dock across from Denman Island. The Thatch
has its own pier, limited to pub-hour use only, for the summer months.

What makes the Thatch Pub unique: view, location, setting, history, architecture, community focus

The simplest of things can sometimes hold the kernel of greatness. The
modest but unique construction of the Thatch Pub, with its "green roof,"
holds a secret. It was one of the earliest designs of famed Vancouver architect Arthur Erickson (1924-2009), who went on to world acclaim with over
500 projects, including Simon Fraser University, the Museum of Glass in Ta-
coma, Wash., and the San Diego Convention Centre (arthurerickson.com).

Sown with sedum, mosses, and grasses, the earthen roofs of the Thatch
are as practical as they are picturesque, keeping the interior cool in summer and warm in winter. Lisa Parnell, whose father, Jack, contracted with
a young Erickson in the '50s to design the buildings on their resort (which
then included cabins and a
store), recalls having to go
atop the roof to mow it.
Today an idle push mower
stands guard amid the
thatch.

Inside, the restaurant and
pub sit side by side, and
outdoors, sprawling decks,
cantilevered over the inter-

(photo courtesy Thatch Pub)

tidal flats, lead one's gaze to the ferry dock and sandy beach below. The interior, with many windows, has seating at the bar and tables and includes a pool table niche. The Teredo wood feature wall is hard to miss and suggests there may be some value to a sea worm of ill repute. Rock features add to the Ericksonian feel. The clapboard exterior and "thatch" roof strike the eye as distinctly island features, especially when viewed in the beach context. The original resort, known then as the Shingle Spit Resort, included a store, restaurant, cabins, home and pub. Renamed the Thatch in the 1970s, it has lost the home and store, but a gift shop and small hotel have been added. This is a place to put in for a stay and allow a full evening enjoying the sunset from the deck.

From the deck, parents can keep watch over children playing on the beach, and travellers can keep an eye on the ferry, which can be spied as it departs from nearby Denman for its 10-minute crossing. Labour Day weekend is special, as, in a farewell gesture to summer known as the Wave Off, the ferry does a mid-channel ballet, with water hoses spraying, perhaps in conjunction with an unclothed whizz-past by a masked maiden and beau from Ford's Cove, saluted by merrymakers on the beach, deck and behind windows. Well worth witnessing on the website. July 1 sees the humorous and popular "build, bail and sail" boat competition.

Entertainment includes a Friday jazz night, a tradition of more than 20 years with the same talented band—all accomplished local musicians. It is popular enough that a water taxi provides return service from Comox. The Vancouver Island craft brewing flag is carried on tap, along with Cumberland Brewing. In the works is a Hornby Island shuttle bus to offer connections to many places of interest, including three wineries, a meadery, distillery, studios, beaches, hikes and more. Whether stretched out on the grass; propped up on the deck, watching the busy beach and water world below; or inside, courtesy of the large windows, watching a vibrant sunset while listening to accomplished jazz strains, the Thatch is an easy place to be.

Earning your beer
Hornby and nearby Denman Island have more than enough to make them a destination vacation. Thatch patrons can work up an appetite with the 45-minute waterside and forest trail to Ford's Cove, which offers a little coffee shop, tours, rentals and mooring. About the island are exceptional parks, such as Helliwell, with its stunning cliff-top hike, broad Tribune Bay with its white sand beach, Mount Geoffrey Nature Park, and a network of destination mountain biking trails.

ESTABLISHMENT 6 2

Cumberland Brewing Company

2732 Dunsmuir Avenue, Cumberland
1-250-400-2739
Webpage – cumberlandbrewing.com
Services – wi-fi, wheelchair-accessible with wheel chair-accessible washrooms

Location
Dunsmuir Avenue, in the heart of Cumberland

What makes Cumberland Brewing unique: craft brewery, business model and community focus

If you build it, they will come! And Cumberland Brewing has done just that. Working on the premise that a small brewery can be very successful serving only a local catchment area and having their customers, commercial and individual, pick up their beer on site, Cumberland Brewery has both enhanced its operation and expanded in its relatively brief existence.

Founders Darren Adam, Michael Tymchuk, and Caroline Tymchuk strongly believe that a community-focused business that treats its employees and customers well and gives back to its community can thrive in a relatively small market. For them, that market is the Comox Valley, with few exceptions.

Housed in a boxy, utilitarian building, where the workings of the brewery share space with a limited public seating area, it manages to create an atmosphere of welcome and character. Its indoor capacity of 49 is is supplemented by a semi-

sheltered patio that can be used year-round, thanks to outdoor heaters. The family-friendly atmosphere is part of the place's welcoming community feel.

Eye-catching adornments include a wave sculpted of wood in the patio area, a growing collection of empty "growlers" from various places, and a chandelier crafted of metal. There is also a "Beer it Forward" board, where people can fund a favour in appreciation for thoughts or deeds done.

The ideal of doing favours for the community is reflected in the pub's ongoing financial support for the Cumberland Community Forest Society, a group committed to saving the surrounding forest. Sponsoring fundraisers and committing a per-litre donation from production of their Forest Fog brew is the company's way of showing community commitment.

Which brings us to the beer. The five regular beers on tap, which include an Oatmeal stout (the Dancing Linebacker), Finally IPA, Red Tape Pale Ale, Just a Little Bitter English Bitter and unfiltered Wheat Ale Forest Fog, are complemented by three rotating taps, which have dispensed 41 different recipes since the brewery opened in 2015. The brewery is forever experimenting with new and novel ingredients. Believing craft beer making is all about integrity, the brew masters use no ingredients intended to reduce the costs of production. The creativity here extends to the menu philosophy, which is to send the customer away with the feeling he or she has just had an exceptional experience.

The place and people exude creativity, commitment and community connection. But if you want to experience the brews, you must come to the Comox Valley.

Earning your beer

In addition to hiking and biking in the Cumberland area proper, you are only a half-hour drive on Highway #19 from the wealth of activities at famed Mount Washington (mountwashington.ca). In winter, there is both alpine and nordic skiing, while summer features hiking, mountain biking and chair lift rides.

ESTABLISHMENT 6 3

The Waverley Hotel

2692 Dunsmuir Avenue, Cumberland
                     1-250-336-8322
Webpage –   waverleyhotel.ca
Services –   wi-fi, wheelchair-accessible with wheel chair-accessible washrooms

Location
On Dunsmuir Avenue, in the heart of Cumberland

What makes the Waverley unique: history, architecture, music, number of craft taps and ghosts (?)

Like the community of which it is an integral part, "The Wave" has risen again after a long ebb in the former coal-mining town, which is quickly reinventing itself. Beginning life as a temperance (non-drinking) boarding house in the early 1880s, it did not begin to encourage imbibing until after Prohibition in 1920. The original building swallowed up its commercial neighbour, Cheap John's, and in 1964 survived a fire that led to the loss of the top floor and subsequent renovations. There have been many face-lifts over the years, including more than a few by long-time owner Harvey Brown, who ran the Wave from 1983 to 2011. He has many a story to tell and still frequents the premises as a patron.

The interior features two levels, incorporating a dance floor and music stage. And it is an amply used stage, with live music Thursday through Saturday—mostly dance music with a rock 'n' roll flavour, but also an eclectic mix of genres. Initially Brown's brainchild, the stage has been graced with likes of Corb Lund, Maria Muldaur, Eliot Brood, Delhi to

Dublin, and Mother, Mother, to name a few. Historic and personal artifacts dot the woody interior. Old bottles and antlers, a metal crow made by a patron, a wood carving of a miner, an inherited chiming clock that Harvey brought back to life, a bicycle hanging from the ceiling to complement one above the entranceway, a hanging chairlift and a host of historic photos of the hotel and long-gone locals are all reminders of the passage of time and people.

It was a tough place in its day, and it was Harvey who imposed a no-fighting rule that took time and tribulation to effect. He referred to the Waverley as the "Hug and Slug," recalling that patrons would enter with hugs for each other and end the evening with punch-ups.
And if these walls have stories to tell, could it be there are ghosts who recall them, too? Some believe the ghost of onetime caretaker Gary still hangs around.

The Wave owns 17 taps, with all but one dedicated to craft beers, and two rotating taps. Island craft breweries represented include Cumberland, Phillips, Vancouver Island, Hoyne, Longwood, and Courtenay's own Gladstone. A tip to the traditionalists is draft Guinness, along with taps for wine and cider. A varied and exceptional menu complements the brews.

There is good daytime bus service and safe-ride options to complement the local taxis in the evenings. The Wave also encompasses a couple of hotel rooms and a liquor store. Along the wall of the store is an intriguing mural. Former employee Gillian Brooks used lights to create silhouettes of real people in a party scene and incorporated them into the mural of a setting sun against a forested mountain backdrop. But it is a rising sun that shines on Cumberland these days, and the Waverley continues to be very much a part of that sunrise.

Earning your beer
Cumberland has become a mecca for mountain bikers, with miles upon miles of trails in the surrounding forest. The trails are also available to hikers, but caution is important, given that this is bear country, and it's suggested that hikers use bear bells or hike in groups. An interesting option is to do a walkabout of the town and the length of Dunsmuir Avenue, with its historic plaques telling the story of the mining town. Trails lead to the site of the old and once very large Chinatown, though no buildings survive. The museum is just down the road from the Waverley.
It is a little town with a lot going on.

ESTABLISHMENT 64

Cornerstone Cafe & Taphouse

208 5th Street, Courtenay
1-250-871-8988
Webpage – cornerstonetaphouse.com
Services – wi-fi, wheelchair-accessible with wheel chair-accessible washrooms

<u>Location</u>
Downtown Courtenay, at the corner of Cliffe and 5th Street

<u>What makes Cornerstone unique:</u> number of craft beers on tap, art events

Just a a cornerstone is foundational to a building, the gathering place built upon it can be foundational to a community. Cornerstone Cafe and Taphouse was envisioned by the owners of Gladstone Brewery as a place where they could support the broader craft beer industry by carrying a wide assortment of craft beer products, along with wines and ciders. This collaboration is inspired by a desire to connect with the community through offering arts events and supporting local business.

The building was originally the multi-storey Lavers Department Store, the oldest department store in town, which became a coffee shop in the 1980s. In 2016, Cornerstone Taphouse took over, inheriting customers from the old coffee shop and enticing new patrons. In a testament to continuity, the Lavers still own the building.

Cornerstone, with its spaciousness and high ceilings, presents a contemporary and welcoming atmosphere, with communal seating and individual tables and bar

stools accommodating solo folks. Large windows bathe the interior in natural light. Service is British style, meaning you go to the bar to order food and drink. And the Taphouse is family-friendly, with no age restrictions.

The 32 taps are the most this side of Victoria and dispense 20 rotating craft beers (two of which are dedicated to American craft beers), eight wines (B.C. wines from the Okanagan and the Island), two ciders and two types of kombucha (a non-alcoholic beverage). The pub is always on the lookout for new and rare craft beers. On the day we visited, there were beers and ciders from Victoria, Portland, Delta, Gibsons, Port Moody, Courtenay, Chemainus, Sooke, and the Cowichan Valley. Four-glass sampler flights are available.
Highly focused on food, the pub makes a point of ensuring all dishes include some local product.

The desire to connect with the community extends to the art events featured here. In addition to Friday music (mostly acoustic), there are poetry and author readings, along with a vinyl night, when patrons bring in their vinyl albums for play. Of particular note is the artist spotlight night, when an artist creates a piece on site and it is auctioned off to patrons afterward.

A bus interchange is within eyesight of the Taphouse.
Location, function, and philosophy all suggest that the name Cornerstone was well chosen.

Earning your beer
About a two-kilometre walk away is Puntledge Park, abutting the Puntledge River. Here, there are easy nature trails and places to relax alongside the river: an attraction for adult swimmers and those who enjoy river floating.

ESTABLISHMENT **65**

Gladstone Brewing Company

Unit A, 244 4th Street, Courtenay
     1-250-871-1111

Marketing Manager –	Marissa Johnson
Owner –	Daniel Sharratt
Webpage –	gladstonebrewing.ca
Hours –	11 a.m. to midnight daily
Services –	wi-fi, wheelchair-accessible with wheel chair-accessible washrooms

<u>Location</u>
Downtown Courtenay

<u>What makes Gladstone Brewing unique:</u> brewery, theme, setting

They say that to get where you are going you must remember whence you came. Gladstone Brewing Company does so in name and theme.

Having begun life in a garage on Gladstone Avenue in Victoria, its re-location to a Courtenay heritage building that once housed the 1940s-era Seale and Thomson garage was only fitting. The garage theme is carried through inside, featuring handmade tap handles created from vintage mechanic's tools, beer flights served on vintage licence plates, and a room scattered with 1940s-era oil cans, hubcaps and toolboxes. The Filling Station is a room devoted to filling growlers, while the Tasting Room is for exactly that.

The brews, which have garnered awards, focus on their flagship Belgian ales, European lagers and Pacific Northwest–style

India pale ales. All to be savoured in the small indoor section, accommodating 30, or the welcoming, partially sheltered outdoor patio, which seats up to 120. The patio is in use year-round, thanks to outdoor heaters. Plans are to eventually cover the entire patio.

The patio abuts a treed square shared with surrounding businesses. It's the site of various events, such as the Springtober Fest, for which Gladstone becomes the unofficial beer garden. Musical entertainment is offered year-round within the patio area.
Minors are allowed with parents, and so are well-behaved dogs and their owners.

Those interested can head indoors to witness the brewing process and savour air laden with the smell of fresh hops.

As the pub is located in downtown Courtenay, the setting is abuzz with people.

The old heritage building has known many uses over the years, but probably none so inviting and refreshing.

Earning your beer
The Gladstone Brewing Company is only a couple of blocks away from the start of the lengthy Courtenay River Walk, which begins at 6th Street. Its wheelchair-friendly paved pathway leads through commercial and residential areas before sidling up beside the river. It wends through parks and viewpoints along the way, opening to vistas of the broad river mouth.

ESTABLISHMENT 66

The White Whale Public House

975 Comox Road, Courtenay

	1-250-338-1468
Webpage –	whitewhalecourtenay.ca
Services –	wi-fi

Location
On Comox Road, between the 5th Street and 17th Street bridges, after crossing the Courtenay River from downtown Courtenay.

What makes the White Whale unique: history, setting, view, range of craft beers

Legend has it the First Nations peoples of the Comox Valley, fleeing the rising waters of a great flood, were saved when Queneesh, the Comox Glacier, released itself from the land to become a great raft upon which the people floated to safety. Afterwards, it returned to its lofty perch, and the legend of the white whale was born.
If you tie yourself to a legend, it had best be a good one. Perhaps that is one reason the White Whale Pub has what owner Max Oudendag refers to as "good energy."

Starting life as a naval toll house on the Courtenay Slough, which was dredged out by the navy, the building went through incarnations as a residence, French restaurant La Cremaiere, and 16 years as the Monte Cristo pub, before settling in over the past few years as the White Whale.

Tall and Tudor-styled, it sits elegantly alongside the tranquil tidal slough, looking across at pastoral Simms Park. Its 80-foot dock is an inviting put-in for small boats,

(photo courtesy White Whale)

paddleboards, canoes and kayaks. The broad outer patio drinks in the setting, comfortably accommodating 60 patrons without sacrificing atmosphere.

The Tudor theme extends to the interior, where niches and more communal settings allow for groups large or small to be comfortably accommodated: up to 120 persons. A low-key, family-friendly atmosphere is fundamental to the philosophy of the White Whale, as is a sense of connecting with the surrounding community in its menu offerings.

An extensive list of local suppliers for food and beverage reveals how seriously this goal is pursued. Then there are the 16 taps, of which all but two are rotating, and all are craft beers or ciders. Trying four samplers at a given time, presented on paddles carved in the form of a whale, is an inviting option with so many to chose from. On the day we visited, products from Delta, Vancouver, Kelowna, Victoria, Nanaimo, Saanichton, Cumberland, Campbell River, Powell River, and Surrey were represented. There is also a sizeable selection of non-alcoholic beverages. The philosophy here includes a desire to champion new businesses, and in particular new craft beer endeavours, so don't be surprised to find "new kids on the block" on tap.

Sitting on the deck on a sunny day, soaking in the setting, enjoying a fine meal and a sampler paddle of beers, it's easy to sense the "good energy" of the White Whale. And the great glacier knowingly smiles down upon its namesake.

Earning your beer
It is a brief walk to the short trail leading around Simms Park, which offers some viewing platforms overlooking the slough and river and also connects to a longer walk under the highway to Lewis Park, where there is river access (popular among floaters), tennis courts, and an outdoor swimming pool.

For more water-oriented activities, there are canoe, kayak and SUP (Stand Up Paddleboard) rentals available at Comox Valley Kayaks in Courtenay. (comoxvalleykayaks.com; 1-888-545-5595).

Paddling upriver and into the slough for a meal and brew would make for quite a day.

ESTABLISHMENT 6 7

Blackfin Pub at the Marina

132 Port Augusta Street, Comox
                          1-250-339-5030
Webpage –   blackfinpub.com
Services-   wi-fi, wheelchair-accessible with wheel
                          chair-accessible washrooms

Location
Right off Comox Road (deep in the heart of Comox) on Port Augusta Street, leading to the marina.

What makes the Blackfin unique: view, craft beer, location, setting, decor

A black dorsal fin erupting from the blue Pacific waters set against a glaciered mountain backdrop emphatically says coastal British Columbia. What better symbol for a pub resting above a marina, opening to a bay with a vista of the Comox Glacier?

Don't let the "Please Wait to be Seated" sign and the rich quality decor fool you when you walk through the front door; this is a casual, welcoming place, at home with cycling attire as much as a suit jacket, and every bit a cornerstone of the community. Its walls are adorned with the works of local artists, and the downstairs banquet room is occasionally employed as a gallery for local talent. Walking clubs, cycling clubs, and dragonboaters, to name but a few, frequent the woody confines of the inner sanctum or spend time on the open-air deck, gazing out over the marina and the snowy smile of the Comox Glacier amid the Island's Beaufort Mountain Range.

Opened in 1989 on the site of the old Elks Hotel, which had burned down a few decades ago, it, too,

(photo courtesy Black Fin)

suffered the ravages of fire in 1991. But it was rebuilt in quality style, using cherrywood and Honduras mahogany. The interior was opened up with large windows that now wash patrons with light and vista. A convincing natural-gas fireplace ensconced in a hearth warms the place, while hanging above it is the Boston-designed Whitehall Boat, built in Sidney. These boats were of a type favoured as water taxis in the early 19th century. But this keel has yet to taste water. Incorporated in the setting is a nautical helm at least 75 years old but of unknown provenance, with a view of the marina below. Seating allows for groups of varying sizes, with niche seating providing for greater privacy and the outer deck open for panoramic appreciation.

The warm, woody interior suggests quality construction and care here, even though the atmosphere is one of casual comfort. Of the 17 taps, nine are occupied by Vancouver Island craft beer products, dispensing the brews of Phillips, Lighthouse, Hoyne, and Driftwood breweries, plus the pub's own special brew, Blackfin Lager, by Vancouver Island Brewery, which is presented in glasses etched with an orca. These are complemented by the local products of Courtenay's Gladstone Brewing Company and Cumberland Brewing Company. And, to keep George Orwell happy, there is Guinness on tap.

Plus, if you want to tap into the view from afar, the website features a webcam overlooking the marina and mountains. As you sit back on a sunny day, gazing out over the bay, marina (with its fishing fleet), and Comox Glacier, it would not be out of place for a black fin to break the water's surface and tip its dorsal in salute.

Earning your beer
The Blackfin is walking and biking distance from the tree-shaded vale of the Brooklin Creek trail and Mack Laing Nature Park, which opens on the waters and salt marshes of the bay. Hikers, birders and naturalists can while away hours here. Not far distant is Goose Spit Point and open views across to the Coast Mountain Range of the mainland. Cheek by jowl lies downtown Comox, worthy of exploration in its own right and complete with green-painted cycling lanes for those favouring wheels over feet. The annual Filberg Festival, with its music and unique market, is foot distance away. The marina and bay are a hive of activity, with annual dragonboat races, paddleboard competitions, sailing club exercises. , and, every second year, the Van Isle 360 sailboat racers putting in here as part of their grand course around the Island.

ESTABLISHMENT 68

The Griffin Pub

1185 Kimorley Road, Comox

1-250-339-4466

Webpage: griffinpub.ca

Services –   wi-fi, wheelchair-accessible with wheel chair-accessible washrooms

Location

On Kimorley Road, on the way to Kin Beach; just to the right off of Little River Road, running alongside the fenced airport property

What makes the Griffin unique: setting, location, theme, view

The legendary griffin is a fusion of the eagle and the lion, king of both birds and beasts, and the eternal guardian of great treasures and priceless possessions. Here, what's being guarded is a golden reputation, rather than boxes of gold.

The Griffin Pub prides itself on comfort and community, tied to the theme of aviation amid the aura of an olde-style English pub. Walls adorned with aviation photos spanning many a year, coupled with open-beam supports, wood wainscotting, dartboards, a pool table, and English memorabilia can put one in mind of pubbing in the days of the Battle of Britain. The Tudor-style entrance is guarded by a stoic knight, whose story allegedly began with a garage-sale purchase and the title Sir Percy, and the emblazoned Griffin only adds to the image. The spacious interior offers room for groups large and small, providing a sense of coziness even though it embraces larger numbers.

The aviation theme comes easily here; the Griffin is next to the Comox airfield; patrons can laze about on the expansive outdoor patio and drink in what's

happening in the sky above. It may be the graceful rise of gliders, the buzz of military craft, or even training sessions of the famed Snowbirds. Night lights enhance the evening atmosphere. This is an ideal spot from which to watch the air shows that happen in Comox, while its secluded setting provides for views of the odd deer grazing lazily nearby.

If memories hang heavy on the walls, they rest more lightly on the pub's remembrances of past patrons, such as one Mark Hendrickson, whose old bar chair carries a plaque that says, "Hairy Little Bastard—This Bud's For You." There's also Penguin's chair and Jen's bench (in memory of a much-loved bartender). A three-level rack of legacy currencies runs the length of the valance above the bar.

A number of Vancouver Island craft breweries are on tap, as is Guinness. Wednesdays, there's a piano bar, on Fridays a live band with no cover charge, and Saturdays feature "Name That Tune." Regular events include the annual Glacier Golf Tournament, Alexander Keith's Birthday (Oct. 5), a Cinco De Mayo celebration and Saint Patrick's Day. A sense of community responsibility here extends to providing a shuttle service for patrons seven days a week. The years have ticked by successfully since the pub began operating in the mid-1980s, suggesting the Griffin guards its reputation well.

Earning your beer

Taking in the busy overhead entertainment is a worthy experience in its own right, but there is more to do close by. Within a short bike ride or a healthy walk is the Comox Air Force Museum, offering a wealth of things to see and learn via displays, videos, and recordings, as well a field of decommissioned planes and helicopters (comoxairforcemuseum.ca). You will come away with a renewed sense of Canada's significant air force contributions and an appreciation for what it has accomplished. Enough, perhaps, to prompt a donation to the museum, which receives no outside funding.

Within a half-hour walk, Air Force Beach opens up the Salish Sea (Georgia Strait) and views of the coastal mountains. You can stroll the beach, soak up the sun, and watch the passing parade of sea craft, airplanes, ferries, and shorebird life. Alongside sits the Teepee Campground, for those inclined to pitch a tent. Regular season runs from March 28 to the October long weekend (250-339-5271). Also nearby is Kin Beach Provincial Park, off Astra Road, with its own campground.

ESTABLISHMENT **69**

Salmon Point Restaurant & Pub

2176 Salmon Point Road, Campbell River
1-250-923-7272
Webpage – salmonpointrestaurant.com
Services – wi-fi, wheelchair-accessible with wheel
chair-accessible washrooms

Location
Just north of the Oyster River, on Salmon Point Road

What makes Salmon Point unique: view, setting, location, marina, closeness to the water and the pub-to-pub hike.

With a patio set so close to the salt chuck that a fish was thrown up to it one particularly stormy day, this is a natural spot to enjoy storm-watching in comfort. With its view encompassing the mainland mountains and the islands between, the expansive Salmon Point Pub is a natural draw for those seeking saltwater ambience, dramatically heightened during stormy weather. Whales, dolphins, sea lions, and orcas share the horizon with passing cruise ships and busy sport craft pulling in catches. The denizens of the deep prove most prominent in August, when the pink salmon are running.

Coming on stream during the early days of neighbourhood pubs in 1982, the Salmon Point Restaurant and Pub has prospered and developed an air of refined casualness. The pub, a wing of the restaurant, is bathed in natural light, courtesy of the large windows facing over sea and patio. Light-coloured wood and painted wainscotting contribute to its spacious feel, centred on a brick-surrounded gas

fireplace. There is table and bench seating, with a comfortable sofa nest facing the fireplace. A West Coast maritime atmosphere flavours the interior, with helms, life-savers and their ilk hanging on the walls. Standing sentry on the patio, overlooking the water, is the amber brown body of a dragon and castle carved of wood.

Salmon Point's sprawling exterior lends it a "grand house" flair, complemented by the open patio looking out to sea and the patio of the adjacent restaurant, protected by glass. Seen from afar, Salmon Point stands out against the seaside horizon as if in lonely vigil.

Vancouver Island craft beers on tap include the products of the Vancouver Island and Phillips breweries of Victoria. A shuttle bus service and other alternative travel options are available.

The West Coast contemporary feel of the Salmon Point Pub is fitting in this beach setting, a lone building on a horizon of sea and mountain.

<u>Earning your beer</u>
One of the neatest trails I have come across has to be the pub-to-pub trail between Salmon Point Pub and the historic, currently closed, Fisherman's Lodge Inn, at the mouth of the Oyster River. Formally called the Oyster River Trail, it is a healthy 45-minute journey one way, with much to witness in the process. In particular, Woodhus Slough is a popular bird-watching area that provides beach views and a profusion of spots to stop and drink in the atmosphere and scenery.

For those fit for travel at sea there is, offshore, Mitlenatch Island Nature Provincial Park, a flora and bird sanctuary. It is home to the greatest seabird colony on the Strait of Georgia, hosting birds ranging from glaucous-winged gulls to black oyster catchers, pelagic cormorants, and pigeon guillemots. May and June are said to offer some of the best times for viewing and photographing plants and birds. Check env.gov. bc.ca/bcparks/explore/parkpgs/mitlenatch_is
The pub's location also puts it close to Miracle Beach Provincial Park and popular Saratoga Beach.

Check out campbellrivertourism.com for more information and suggestions.

ESTABLISHMENT 70

Landing Pub and Grill

629 Quathiaski Cove Road, Quadra Island
1-250-285-2701
Services – wi-fi, wheel chair accessible with wheel
chair accessible washrooms

Location
At the head of Quathiaski Cove, immediately after disembarking from
the Campbell River Ferry.

What makes the Landing unique: setting, view (sunsets), interior, dog-
friendly, atmosphere and history

Built on the site of an original homestead and incorporating its old
chimney, the Landing has evolved from the original small restaurant
into a logging and fishing–themed pub especially beloved of canines
and those who love them.

The vertical-board exterior gives little hint of the log cabin–like interior,
with its rough-hewn log post-and-beam construction, cedar walls, and
wood slat floors. The wheelhouse-style circular bar separates two sections, allowing one side to accommodate families during the daytime
and the other, adults only. In the evening, it is all adult, with the division providing a sense of personal space for all. The old homestead
chimney is guarded on each side by stained-glass fixtures and a photo
of the island ferry, in a setting with ample space and niche seating. The
interior, done in heavy
woods, has a high ceil-
ing and lots of windows
to give it a relaxed feel.
There is a separate en-
tertainment room with a
pool table and darts.

Giving the place an iden-
tity, the walls are adorned
with historic photos and

others of fishing boats, such as that of the BC Packers #45 fishing boat (now housed in the museum in Campbell River) once featured on the Canadian five-dollar bill, which operated out of Quathiaski Cove. These pictures reflect the maritime history of the community, which still has a serious commercial fishing fleet at anchor within view of the pub's windows and deck. There is also a wall of remembrance, known by other names as well, for patrons who have gone on to the big pub in the sky. The hallway to the washrooms has a vibrant underwater seascape mural in which the Beatles' Yellow Submarine would not be out of place.

In summer, the busyness of the tourist season is amplified by folks coming over for events such as the Quadra Palooza music festival, art studio weekends, the annual mixed slow-pitch tournament (which draws around 30 teams), the fall fair, and the Landing's own summer blues jam, which once attracted the regular attendance of a blue heron who regularly arrived for the performance and rested, listening, until it ended. He was, aptly, named Mr. Blue. Alas, Mr. Blue managed to electrocute himself. But another heron was quick to take his place.

On the outside deck is the doggie pub park where man's best friend can sit on an adjacent deck in full view of his master, all within compliance of the health laws. Great idea!

The Landing has a place for everyone, from the avian to the canine to the great sweating masses—and all this with a view.

Earning your beer

Local fishing guides operate out of the cove, and Quadra Island has more than enough activities to foster lengthy vacations: a golf course (quadragolf.com), kayak tours and rentals (quadraislandkayaks.com), bike touring (quadraislandcycle.com) coupled with hiking opportunities, rock climbing, diving and more (quadraislandtourism.ca).

ESTABLISHMENT 71

Heriot Bay Inn

673 Hotel Road, Heriot Bay, Quadra Island

1-888-605-4545

Webpage –   heriotbayinn.com

Services –   limited wi-fi

Location

At Heriot Bay, beside the ferry dock for the ferry to Cortes Island. It is 13 kilometres from the ferry dock for Campbell River at Quathiaski Cove.

What makes the Heriot Bay Inn unique: setting, location, view, hauntings, architecture, history

There is an aura around places that stand solitary for many years against a background of forest, amid the ocean's serenade. Heriot Bay Inn, standing in one form or another since 1895, is just such a place.

In that year, Hosea Arminus Bull first put nail to board. Some 113 years later, his legacy remains in the hands of local islanders, now numbering 21, who have maintained and enhanced this lynchpin of the community. Today, a pub, restaurant, hotel, cabins and mooring are available to visitors by sea and land.

In 1910, the first edifice fell to flames. It was quickly rebuilt in 1911, only to burn again. Once more rising from the ashes in 1912, it has since more than survived the years; the rebuilt structure now comprises the central part of today's inn. Hosea held on until 1926, two years after his wife died, before letting his creation pass to other hands. Hosea may be gone, but other vestiges of the past linger within the inn's walls. Two ghosts

(photo courtesy Heriot Bay Inn)

are said to keep vigil, though their stories and identities remain unknown. A sad lady has been seen knitting in a chair or wandering in apparent expectation of a husband fated never to return. She has revealed a more dynamic side in her need, on occasion, to move furniture about. In the upstairs hallway, the presence of a man is more felt than visualized, the belief being he is the restless soul of a man murdered—or one who committed such an act. Both appear benign.

The pub, with its rough posts, wood panelling, memorabilia, maps and historic photos, is warmly welcoming. A huge photo of Quadra Island's own BC Packers #45 fishing boat, an image of which once graced the back of the Canadian five-dollar bill, dominates one wall, complementing other historical photos. A large Canadian flag stretches across the ceiling before the bar. The stage is shingled with vintage vinyl records and wallpapered with album covers, in homage to the entertainment it regularly hosts. This is a lived-in space, with stories to tell.

The pub is enhanced by a deck that draws the gaze outward and to the grounds of the resort as a whole. With the forest at its back, the pub's seaward view reveals tended gardens, lawns, shrubs, and even a huge chess board with Alice in Wonderland–proportioned playing pieces. An appreciative stroll about the grounds is warranted—a little Eden set within a live wilderness, amid the songs of wind and wash. Long a centre of the community, the inn remains dynamic with open-mic Saturdays, bands on Fridays and, during the winter, special performances in the restaurant, which have featured the likes of Harry Manx and Valdy. A wide range of seating accommodates a substantial number of bottoms on bar stools, benches and at tables. Island craft beer on tap includes two offerings of Victoria's Vancouver Island Brewery.
An island taxi service is available for those who have favoured a brew too many.

Community-owned and -appreciated, the Heriot Bay Inn is a setting to be experienced by new visitors with an ear and eye to longevity, history, and sense of place.

Earning your beer
Nearby and not to be missed is Rebecca Spit Provincial Park, a long lick of a peninsula with a bay to one side and open waters the other. Log-strewn, with a spine trail running its course, this park will never leave you without

a view, including that of the ferry to Cortes crossing Sutil Channel on its 45-minute journey to Whaletown, where visitors have need of neither a car nor a bike. For more hikes, including the nearby Heriot Ride/Gowlland Harbour trail, check quadraislandtrails.ca.

Island events include the Mushroom Festival, Chamber Music in July, May Day Festivities and a Saturday market. The nine-hole island golf course (quadragolf.com) offers a ferry pick-up and drop-off service. The Heriot Bay Inn no longer offers tours, but refers guests to excellent businesses that do. The sheltered bay and beach are ideal for visiting kayakers, while the marina accommodates larger craft. It can prove worthwhile to take the return ferry trip to Cortes Island for the 90-minute sea excursion.

A trip to a First Nations museum, the Nuyumbalees Cultural Centre at the village of Cape Mudge, is more than worthwhile. History and artifacts are brought to life, revealing the richness of an ancient and living culture (museumatcapemudge.com).
For details and more ideas, check out quadraisalnd.com and quadraisland-tourism.ca. There is a visitor information centre at the ferry terminal at Quathiaski Cove.

(photo courtesy Heriot Bay Inn)

ESTABLISHMENT **72**

Rip Tide Marine Pub

1340 Island Highway, Campbell River
1-250-830-0044
Webpage – riptidemarinepub.ca
Services – wi-fi, wheelchair-accessible with wheel
chair-accessible washrooms

<u>Location</u>
In the Discovery Harbour Shopping Centre, facing onto the sea walk.

<u>What makes the Riptide Pub unique:</u> location, view, setting, craft beer list, decor

A long day exploring Campbell River's incredible sea walk has no better break or end than at the Riptide. It's situated conveniently along the walk and serves up an ample view to remind you of your day's trekking while quaffing one of the many Vancouver Island craft beers on tap.

This spacious seaside pub has been drawing mariners and landlubbers to its comfortable and polished quarters since 1997, earning a reputation for its renowned seafood chowder and Vancouver Island–produced craft beer in the process. Offerings include Hoyne, Phillips, Lighthouse, Wolf and Beachfire, all Vancouver Island breweries, along with 10 other taps featuring import and domestic beer. The Riptide manages to be both refined and contemporary without compromising its casual and welcoming flavour.

The dark wood interior rests under a high ceiling, with a cozy central fire pit at the foot of a sweeping central staircase. Lots of large windows allow light to flood into the spacious room, which has ample seating to accommodate everyone from the lone wolf to happy groupings.

Outside, a window-sheltered patio rests alongside the marine walkway. The upper floor sports a niche for groups, focused on a cozy fireplace, where carpeting dampens sound. From here, the crow's-nest view reveals the elegance of the pub, from bar to fireplace to window. Kitty-corner to the pub is the marina, and behind it, all the shopping you need at the Discovery Harbour Shopping Centre.

The Riptide prides itself on its menu and the fact it meets most of its supply needs from local producers. Its menu includes locally caught fish and locally raised shellfish, as well as local organic produce.
The bi-annual Van Isle yacht race participants put over at the marina in the course of their long island circumnavigation.

Options for alternative transportation are available, sometimes with pick-up and drop-off arrangements, including vehicles, taxi or airport shuttle. The Riptide is a worthy reward for a day spent appreciating Campbell River's waterfront trail, with its location by the walkway and marina, with a grand view of Quadra Island and the distant coast mountains.

Earning your beer
From distant Willow Point, far to the south, intrepid hikers or bikers can plan a full day enjoying a six-kilometre-plus route that proffers ever-changing sea views, sand and pebble beaches tossed with driftwood, fantastically designed chainsaw carvings, interpretive signs, totems, the life of the ocean—cruise ships, orcas, fishers, et al—and perhaps a visit to the Campbell River Museum, close to downtown. Follow the route to the very doorstep of the Riptide and beyond, to Tyee Spit.

A walking map may be obtained from the visitor information centre (1235 Shoppers Row in the Tyee Shopping Centre; 250-286-6901; rivercorp.ca/visitor-centre/campbell-river-visitor-centre).

Compact Campbell River has much more to offer for those who want to put foot to path or pedal, including the trails of Beaver Lodge Forest lands, the Willow Creek Conservation area, and Elk Falls Provincial Park, with its new suspension bridge. This is a community with enough to do to keep visitors on the go for a week.

ESTABLISHMENT 73

Beach Fire Brewing & Nosh House

594 11th Avenue, Campbell River
                    1-250-914-3473
Webpage –   beachfirebrewing.ca
Services –   wi-fi, wheelchair-accessible with wheel
                    chair-accessible washrooms

Location
Near the heart of downtown Campbell River, close to Dogwood and 11th Avenue.

What makes the Beach Fire Brewing Pub unique: daily changing menu, dog-friendly patio, it's a brew pub

Since the days of our most ancient ancestors, the communal fire has brought feelings of security and welcome, a sense of being part of a greater whole. That feeling is still evoked by a beach fire set against the night with the lull of waves for background music.
A subculture in Campbell River embraces the beach fire as a given right to be exercised, with due regard for periods with a high threat of forest fire. That is captured in the logo and philosophy of Beach Fire Brewing.

The brewery was purpose-built in the 1950s for a community co-op cable station and had many commercial incarnations before coming into the hands of Beach Fire Brewing in July 2016.

That November, the doors opened to a spacious, high-ceilinged interior dotted with communal tables, bar seating, smaller tables, and a lounge area. The bar is topped by a mill-sawn slab of western maple and the communal tables with "upcycled" fir. The walls are adorned with eclectic art, some of which is for sale, with the plan being to eventually have a rotating art feature supporting local artists. The dog-friendly outdoor patio occupies a strip out front, and there are plans to add a backdoor patio as well. The dynamic menu sees a wholesale change twice a day and is tapas-style, whereby appetizer plates are designed to be shared among friends. Those friends can include the little people, as the Beach Fire is family-friendly. And all meals are made from scratch; no pre-frozen here.

The pub's own unique beer is featured in four regulars—Beach Blonde Ale, High Tide Pale Ale, Ember Red Ale and, for the Orwellian lovers, Wheelbender Stout—as well as two seasonals. The product is available only on site, where the loyal can fill up their "growlers" or sit for a pint. Kegs and equipment are provided for patrons and selected commercial customers. Eventually, the brewery plans on producing cans. It also carries, on tap, Vancouver Island cider and Quadra Island wine.

A sense of collaboration and community here is reflected in things such as producing a tea-infused beer with a local teahouse and a coffee beer with a local cafe. Sundays feature acoustic music, and there are no TVs to draw attention away from socializing. This is, after all, a communal space geared to the social experience, just as the Beach Fire logo symbolizes. This is a place of welcome.

Earning your beer
A short drive along Highway #19A ties in with Campbell River Road and the way to Elk Falls Provincial Park. Here, you can enjoy a short forest hike from the parking lot and interpretive centre to the awe-inspiring suspension bridge strung across the chasm of the Campbell River, affording dramatic views of Elk Falls. There are many further trails to explore and, for the ambitious, the longer Elk Falls Trail.

Pick up a map from the Tourist Information Centre (visitorcentre.ca, 1-877-286-5705) located near 16th Avenue and Shoppers Row.

The Royal Coachman

84 Dogwood Drive, Campbell River
1-250-286-0231
Webpage –   theroyalcoachmaninn.com
Services –   wi-fi, wheelchair-accessible with wheel
                     chair-accessible washrooms

Location
Highly visible Tudor-style pub on Dogwood Street, between Evergreen Road and 2nd Avenue.

What makes the Royal Coachman unique: British pub theme and garden

It takes a commitment to carry off a theme with true authenticity. The Royal Coachman Inn has achieved that, inside and out.

Originally built across the road in 1978, with a utilitarian exterior but authentic British pub design inside, the Coachman was destined to surpass itself in 1988. The pub moved across the road to its new digs, with a resplendent Tudor-style exterior, complete with shake roof, half-timbered siding, and an even better interior. Not only was the former pub's inner sanctum exactingly duplicated, employing the same designer, it was even more authentic—down to hand-hewn posts and beams.

Expansive and atmospheric, with nooks and crannies to accommodate groups, singles and couples, this is a place where a first-time visitor could be excused for craning his neck and gawking. China plates, photos, horse brasses, carriage lanterns, memorabilia, hunting prints, a huge stuffed fish, and stained glass crowd the sightlines. The grand central room is carpeted, and above soars a pitched ceiling, all in keeping with the heavy woods used in the flooring, wainscotting and ceiling. The invitingly homey pit half-circles the brick-hearth fireplace, made all the more welcoming by its library theme. The furnishings leave one as comfortable as in a private study.

Then, step outside to find a garden gnome's heaven. A fountain gurgles at the centre of a pool ringed with trees, flowers and bushes, and a sheltered gazebo provides a haven from the outside world. This award-winning garden is particularly attractive on a sunny day, providing both shade and light.

Entertainment includes music on Sunday afternoons. Wi-fi is available, as is local bus service. Vancouver Island craft breweries are represented by taps for Vancouver Island Brewery and Phillips, both of Victoria. The Coachman has kept a keen eye focused on quality food service since long before it was common for pubs to do so. It also caters for luncheons and events.

The original pub is now complemented by a coffee shop, Mudslingers (which opens at 8 a.m.), a banquet room, executive meeting room, and nearby liquor store, all holding to the British pub theme in form and decor.

If you can't get to Britain for a beer, the Royal Coachman will offer you a comforting alternative, be that inside or out.

Earning your beer
In addition to everything available in the Campbell River area, the Royal Coachman is particularly close to trailheads for the many paths criss-crossing the Beaver Lodge Forest Lands. Pick up a handy city map, care of the tourist information centre (1235 Shoppers Row, 250-286-6901, Tyee Shopping Centre; rivercorp.ca/visitor-centre/campbell-river-visitor-centre). If you're interested in cycling or hiking, there are enough trails and distance to build a healthy appetite before gracing the doors of the Coachman.

**Editors note: as of July 2018 the Royal Coachman is currently closed but will hopefully re-open under new management

ESTABLISHMENT 75

Merecroft Pub (MVP)

489 Dogwood Street South, Campbell River
1-250-286-4944
Webpage –   mvppub.ca
Services –   wi-fi, wheelchair-accessible with wheelchair-
                                    accessible washrooms

Location
In the Merecroft Village Shopping Centre, on Dogwood Street South

What makes the MVP unique: pioneering brew pub with a panoramic view

There is always a special place for pioneering spirits on the West Coast, and the MVP was one of the early brew pubs, especially for the north Island.
Even though it's lodged in a shopping centre, it has a stunning view when the blinds are up and the Island mountains lie stretched across the horizon.
It began its life in 1996 as the Cog and Kettle, then became part of the Fogg n' Suds franchise until 2000, when its present owners took over. The Fogg n' Suds name was retained until 2003, when it was given the double-barrelled title MVP (Merecroft Village Pub) to identify with the shopping centre but also reference its "Most Valuable Player" ambitions.

Patrons are greeted at the entrance with a look-alike to Rodin's The Thinker carved in wood (on loan from the Campbell River Arts Society). You are welcomed into a spacious, two-floor pub with a high, beamed ceiling and ample seating at

the bar, tables, and long communal tables. At the back is the copper-kettle beer-making apparatus. A pool table and ample TV screens keep sports patrons occupied.

The kettles have been making beers since the beginning and currently are the proud fathers of Maple Leaf Logger, The Village Nut and an IPA. The remaining nine taps include a rotating guest tap.
The MVP is well serviced by transit and taxi and shares its abode with a restaurant, which incidentally has its own wooden carving: a First Nations design.

In this new age of burgeoning craft beer options and new pubs springing up like wildfire, there will always be a special place for those, like the MVP, who paved the way.

Earning your beer
The MVP is close to the Beaver Lodge trails, which can offer hours of happy trekking. Drive west on Merecroft Road to the end and you will come across parking and a starting point for the expansive trails of the Beaver Lodge Forest Lands. It's best to pick up a map first from Campbell River Visitor Centre (1235 Shoppers Row) downtown or Tourism Campbell River & Region (900 Alder Street).

SECTION SIX Sunshine Coast

ESTABLISHMENT 76

Shinglemill Pub, Bistro & Marina

6233 Powell Place, Powell River
1-604-483-3545
Webpage – shinglemill.ca
Services – wi-fi, wheelchair-accessible with wheelchair-accessible washrooms

Location
On Highway #101 from Powell River to Lund, immediately to the right after crossing the bridge above the dam. Powell River is accessed by BC Ferries from Comox on the Island or via Saltery Bay, coming from Sechelt and Vancouver. Pacific Coastal Airlines provides connections to Vancouver.

What makes the Shinglemill unique: setting, history, view, location

Taking its name from the memory of a historic shingle mill that supported its own little community of the same name in the early 1900s, this pub and bistro in a postcard locale evolved into a full-service destination—sheltered, fittingly, under a shake roof. Failed and deteriorating, the site was purchased out of bankruptcy in 1983 and re-created. It reopened in 1986 as a modern pub that has kept a connection with its past.

Set at the narrowing mouth of Powell Lake, not far from the dam that effectively created the lake, the pub gazes out on a stunning vista of lake and soaring mountains that could keep a photographer hanging around for days. The busy lakeside activity can be viewed from the outdoor patio, overlooking the boat ramp, or from

(photo courtesy Shinglemill)

the wide windows of the pub and bistro. The pub is bright and airy, with bar chairs, table and chair seating, plus benches spread around the wood-embellished interior. A welcoming gas fireplace stands as a centrepiece, and historical photos grace both table tops and walls. Locals, dragonboaters and tourists often find their way to its welcoming doors, so conveniently available before or after a day's ventures. The lake is more than just a visual attraction, as attested to by the busy marina and many activities offered along its 32-mile length. Townsite Breweries, Powell River's own craft brewery (townsitebrewing.com; open for visits and tours), is represented on tap.

Wheelchair-accessible, the pub also offers free cab service home for groups over four who call for reservations (conditions apply). Free parking is close by.

Sitting at the Shingle Mill, enjoying its comfortable refinements and Powell River's own craft beer, you can drink in the moods of Mother Nature regardless of season or temperament. This is a place for quiet contemplation of nature's ever-changing art or curious observation of man's interplay with the lake.

Earning your beer
Within walking distance are trails hugging the waterline and connecting with other trails climbing to viewpoints. The Sunshine Coast Trail (sunshinecoast-trail.com), a 180-kilometre trek dotted with cabins that runs from Sarah Point in Desolation Sound to Saltery Bay, offers both shorter day treks or a hardy distance venture. Also check out sunshine-coast-trails.com for other options.

The lake offers swimming, fishing (the Arnold Carlson fishing derby) and dragonboat racing at Mowatt Bay. The pub is at the gateway to an extensive canoeing route, the Powell River Canoe Route, encompassing 57 kilometres (eight lakes and five portages) that can be done in whole (taking about five days) or in shorter segments.

From easy day-tripping options to major out-trips, this is a land that offers it all. For more information check out the visitor information centre at 4760 Joyce Avenue, Powell River, at 877-817-8669 and 604-485-4701; webpage discoverpowellriver.com.

ESTABLISHMENT **77**

The Breakwater Inn Pub

The Historic Lund Hotel, Tla'amin Resorts & Accommodations Inc.
Lund, Sunshine Coast

	1-877-569-3999
Webpage –	lundhotel.com
Services –	wi-fi, wheelchair-accessible with wheelchair-accessible washrooms

<u>Location</u>
Where Highway 101 north from Powell River ends.

<u>What makes the Breakwater Inn Pub unique:</u> setting, location, architecture, history and ghosts

For well over a hundred years, the Lund Hotel has, in one form or another, been the central landmark of this photo-perfect village by the sea, its palm-fronted, ocean-facing front façade seemingly drawn from some southern U.S. plantation. It gazes out to a sea of things to do and see, and is as compelling as it is unique.

The Thulin brothers of Sweden first put roots down here in 1889 and named the settlement and their new hotel after a familiar community in the old country. The hotel got a liquor licence in 1895, and in 1905 the new Malaspina Hotel went up alongside the Lund. When the older hotel fell to fire, the newer kid on the block took on the historic name. For many years, the Lund, and the little village it anchored, survived until it fell into disrepair in the 1990s. In 1999, it was rescued, and the hotel, restaurant and pub gained new life, becoming once again the centre of a vibrant community.

The wide windows on the vista side of the pub and restaurant frame a view overlooking the patio seating on the porch and the green lawn, with its jumbo-sized chess board and a magnificent vista capturing the eye beyond. Ocean, islands, and the distant Vancouver Island mountains rise beyond the busy marina. It's a stunning setting in which to soak up the sun and appreciate beauty.

Inside, the spacious Breakwater pub is bright with sunshine and light wood hues in the flooring, walls, and bar. Seating includes table and chairs, bench and bar, offering options for both the loner and the gathering of the clans. Historic photos dot the walls, and fine carvings adorn the bar. The effect is one of comfortable lightness and space.

In a tip to local flavour, the Breakwater commits three of its taps to Powell River's own Townsite Brewery craft beer products. For those interested, the brewery offers tasting and tours (604-483-2111, townsitebrewingco.com). There is wi-fi in the pub and restaurant, and patron parking is available. The Breakwater is the haunt of respected local long-time customers, who can tell many stories of the pub and its environs. One, Russell, gained a measure of fame in a book by Grant Lawrence, Adventures in Solitude, and is often sought out by tourists for stories and possibly an autograph.

This place is the haunt of others as well. Hotel guests have seen the visage of a man sitting at the end of their bed, only to later recognize him in a photo of the Thulin brothers. A female apparition, attired in a long, old white dress with lace neckline and hemline, frequently passes, never showing her face. Some believe she is the restless spirit of a woman who hanged herself in one of the rooms. The pub manager has often come to work to see the covering on a third-floor window up, only to notice it is down when she leaves—questions arising from the fact that floor is locked, with only a select few holding a key. From that same floor, footsteps and bangs have been heard. Fortunately these apparitions seem to be benign, though one customer fled the pub when, for no apparent reason, some glasses flew off the bar shelf.

One look at the view and setting, and it is easy to see why easygoing old guests would want to hang around.

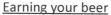

Earning your beer

Don't expect to come here and experience it all in a day. Below the pub, Lund Water Taxi service (lundwatertaxi.com, 604-483-9749) awaits those wishing to travel to the famed sand beaches of Savary Island, the nature reserve of Mitlenach Island, lonely Cortes, famed Desolation Sound, and the starting point of the 180-kilometre Sunshine Coast Trail at Sarah Point. Detailed maps of the trail system are available at the pub and hotel lobby. Adventurers can opt for a short day trip or longer excursions.

The village itself is worth exploring, with boardwalks that hover over the water and many galleries, shops and eateries. The marina hums with pleasure craft, workaday barges, and boats big and small. The place is even more alive on Lund Dayz and during the Shellfish Festival, with booths offering workshops on First Nations weaving, preserved foods, arts and crafts.

Here, where the road ends, it is easy to see why Lund is called the Gateway to Desolation Sound, and the Breakwater Inn pub is the waypost. A special place and a special pub.

ESTABLISHMENT 78

Riggers Pub Style Restaurant

Savary Island

1-604-483-7966

Services -   wi-fi

Location

On the main road, uphill from the dock, a five-minute walk from the water taxi terminal. Access to Savary is via boat or 15-minute water taxi ride from Lund, on the Sunshine Coast just north of Powell River.

What makes Riggers unique: theme, Savary Island, setting and location

Spotted from above, Savary Island, with its virtual circumnavigating beaches, looks like some South Pacific atoll, and its favoured seaside sub-climate only adds to the image. No wonder, then, that this informal, rustic pub with a nautical theme allows patrons to put away their watches and throw off the worries of the world. Set amid field and forest, where the rapping of a busy pileated woodpecker may provide the musical backdrop for a doe fearlessly grazing on the pub grounds, Riggers is an oasis in Paradise.

The original store expanded to include the pub restaurant 20 years ago and now provides three outdoor seating venues (deck, lawn and sheltered porch), plus an eclectically decorated interior space hung with flags, maps, lanterns, plaques, nets, nautical paraphernalia, and

newspaper clippings— for example the tale of a store robbery in the early years that ended in a hanging. Skylights in the open post-and-beam ceiling enhance the bright, wood-finished interior. There is ample choice in seating, in and out, including at the bar or tables. Accentuating the peaceful atmosphere is the fact that Savary is not a destination easily reached, unless you have a boat or take the water taxi from Lund. Services include wi-fi, the only public-use washrooms on the island, and satellite TV. Entertainment includes karaoke nights and, usually, live band nights during summer long weekends. On tap are Powell River's own Townsite craft brewery products. The adjacent store, an important feature as it's the only one on Savary, provides groceries, produce, ice, ice cream, snacks, rope and fresh baking.

Though set amid the trees, Riggers is close enough that you can hear the ocean breathe on its fabled beaches.
It is a place to be experienced and savoured.

Earning your beer
There are few cars using the dirt roads of Savary Island, as they must be barged over, so you'll have little concern for traffic as you explore the island. Pick up a map from the water taxi office in Lund and probe the trails leading to long sandy beaches and vast views, east and west. Keep your eyes open for both beach and sea as you stroll along these uncrowded trails for as long as you want, provided you keep a watch on the tide.

The network of roads gives more than enough opportunity to explore the island and check out the eclectic houses here, ranging from a simple cottage to grander homes, including a very compelling log residence turned into a B&B. There is ample space where nature reigns supreme, and birders can search foliage, beach and horizon for their winged quarry. There are trails down to the north beach, with its warm swimming waters and the forever-posing mermaid statue watching from its rock. The south beach, which sometimes offers glimpses of sunning seals or sea lions as well as providing warm swimming waters, is accessed via the steep Sutherland Stairs.

Near Riggers, set in the trees, is a quaint non-denominational chapel that has stood open to all for some 20 years. Popular in the summer and subject to ferry and water taxi demand, Savary Island takes some planning to experience. It's best to check out water taxi information at lundwatertaxi.com, where you can also pick up a map of the island.

SECTION SEVEN West Coast

ESTABLISHMENT 79

The Eagle's Nest Pub

1990 Bay Street, Ucluelet

1-250-726-7570

Webpage – islandwestresort.com

Services – wi-fi, wheelchair-accessible with wheelchair-accessible washrooms

Location

Coming into Ucluelet, turn left off the main road (Peninsula Road–Highway #A4) onto Bay Street, and follow it to the bottom, turning left into the pub's parking lot, overlooking the docks.

What makes the Eagle's Nest unique: view, location, setting, marina and the eagles

It seems nature's denizens are as comfortable here as the Eagle's Nest's patrons. The dynamic views from its many windows and wrap-around deck range from statuesque great blue herons holding vigil on the docks to barking sea lions, eagles, singular or in throngs, the occasional orca, curious seals, and, in the summer, the bustle of sport fishing boats bringing in their catches, much to the delight of the gulls. All this is set against the green-clad skirts of the mountains across the the bay, which include Mount Ozzard, namesake of the pub's tasty Ozzard Burger. The pub comes by its name honestly, as there is an eagle's nest in the trees behind.

The striking photos adorning the walls, creations of bar supervisor Sherrie Pawluk, are in keeping with the setting and location, the most notable being a close-up of an immature bald eagle sufficiently at ease to allow the photographer to come in close for a good shot.

(photo courtesy Sherrie Pawluk)

The bright, open and spacious interior, done in rich woods, is fully wrapped by an outside deck that has two areas where dogs can be leashed within a comforting view of their masters while abiding with health regulations. Inside, high ceilings and a wealth of windows bathe the two seating levels with natural light. The space incorporates an area for a pool table and another for a dance floor. The summer Wednesday-night jams featuring local talent are popular and get folks participating in both playing and dancing. Children are welcome until 8 p.m.

Seating for 100 inside includes both table-and-chair options and bar seating. Tofino's own brewery products are on tap. The pub is part of a larger complex, including a marina, pet-friendly motel, camping and RV sites. Drawing patrons regularly are fishing derbies and the horde of activities Ucluelet offers, winter and summer.
This is a peaceful place during the day to dine and watch nature go about its business in the waters and sky.

Earning your beer
Ucluelet is not large, and the Eagle's Nest is within walking distance of the Wild Pacific Trail across the peninsula. The Big Beach to Ancient Cedars trail is a five-kilometre stroll one way, providing dramatic views of beach and rocks, alive with crashing waves spraying high into the air and serenading you with their constant roar. It even has sectioned Artist Loops, which are self-explanatory once you experience their vistas. A second trail, the 2.6-kilometre Lighthouse Loop, is at the far south end of the peninsula.

Pick up a handy Tofino/Ucluelet map from the visitors centre on Peninsula Road. It offers maps of Tofino and Ucluelet, plus the long stretch of the world-famed Pacific Rim National Park Reserve in between. Here, nature is ever present, be it forest or sea. To the south, the Broken Islands Chain is famed for kayaking, and Canada's surfing capital beaches lie just to the north. Kayak tours and rentals, whale-watching and adventure cruises and numerous beaches complement the hiking. A place for artists and photographers to lose themselves. Ucluelet boasts its own aquarium and a host of events, including Ukee Days, the Edge to Edge Marathon (half-marathon and relay), the Paddle the Edge kayak competition, and the Whale Festival (March). It's a put-in for the Van Isle 360, a yacht race circumnavigating Vancouver Island. There are many reasons Ucluelet is a destination site and a growing attraction.

For more details, check out ucluelet.ca and pacificrimwhalefestival.com

ESTABLISHMENT 80

The Hatch Waterfront Pub

634 Campbell Street, Tofino, Tofino Resort & Marina
1 -844-680-4184
Webpage –   tofinoresortandmarina.com
Services –   wi-fi, wheelchair-accessible with wheelchair-accessible washrooms

<u>Location</u>
Seaside, just as you enter Tofino, earmarked by a large white building (motel front desk) advertising the Tofino Resort + Marina. Both pub and adjoining 1909 Kitchen restaurant are highlighted on the sign.

<u>What makes The Hatch unique:</u> view, setting, marina and location

Sitting by one of the large windows here, facing out upon Clayoquot Sound and cantilevered over the water, is like experiencing a large-screen HD 3D TV screen—only this is the real thing. Constant action passes before your eyes, with float planes landing and taking off, herons patrolling the marina wharf below, otters playing, seals popping up curious heads, eagles wheeling, fishing boats putting in and out, fisherman hauling ashore their catches and cleaning, much to the delight of hovering gulls.

Whether on the broad outside patios, with their heaters to extend the season and temper cool days, or in the interior bathed in natural light (courtesy of the wealth of large windows taking up the full extent of the seaward walls), you are never far from a harbour view. Built with raw post-and-beam construction, the pub is expansive and spacious, with a range of seating from bar to bench to table and chairs. It ex-

udes an upscale but inviting atmosphere. The popular pool room niche accompanies the large main room, on the other side of the long, horseshoe bar.

Closed from December 2016 until May 2017, the former Jack's Waterfront Pub went through major renovations that added an upstairs pub section complete with its own deck, along with the 1909 Kitchen restaurant, also with its own deck. Despite its total capacity of 350, no one is ever far away from the magnificent views. The upstairs pub can also be used as a banquet room.

It is all a part of the larger marina complex, which includes the marina and hotel. The complex is involved in local fishing derbies and sponsors its own Fishing for the Future event with major prizes, and profits going to charity. From its docks depart fishing charters, whale- and bear-watching tours, and hot-springs excursions. Of the 14 copper taps downstairs and four upstairs, all are dedicated to B.C. beer products and most to Island-produced suds. Phillips (Victoria), Tofino, Hoyne (Victoria) and Driftwood (Victoria) are all well represented. While Guinness does not enjoy a tap, Tofino's Kelp Stout and Hoyne's Honey-dark Matter fill the void. Thursday nights are reserved for live music.

Still exploring new ideas, the pub's ambition is to have a different element of food or beverage featured each day of the week.
The entertainment here never ceases. You need only take a seat by a window or out on one of the decks to be surrounded with a living sea world framed by big skies and forest.

Earning your beer
So where do you begin with things to do and see in Tofino? Perhaps a water taxi to hike on Meares Island or an excursion to whale-watch or enjoy seaside hot springs; or perhaps a boat trip to see the haunt of famed "Cougar Annie." The renowned West Coast beaches of nearby Pacific Rim National Park are an international draw. The area remains a destination for surfers, photographers, divers, kayakers, hikers, bird watchers, cyclists and their ilk. Tofino is an Eden for the reflective as much as the active. To emphasize the significance of this scenic setting, Clayoquot Sound has been established as a UNESCO Biosphere Reserve sheltering more than 647,000 acres of the largest temperate rainforest left on Earth.
Check clayoquotbiosphere.org for information.

ESTABLISHMENT 81

Wolf in the Fog

150 Fourth Street, Tofino

	1-250-725-9653
Webpage –	wolfinthefog.com
Services –	wi-fi, wheelchair-accessible downstairs

Location
Conspicuous at Fourth and Campbell Streets, shortly after entering town.

What makes Wolf in the Fog unique: location, atmosphere, artisan liquors, decor, philosophy and view

In a place where atmosphere hangs like the anticipated crash of a monster wave, Wolf in the Fog is a fit in philosophy and feeling. At once modern and creative in both food and drink, it ties itself to the foreverness of this place, drawing locally from both land and sea. The mantra "fish, forage and feast" governs this new-kid-on-the-block establishment, which skyrocketed to national acclaim within weeks of opening. It was listed as #1 in the top-ten new restaurants in Canada by Air Canada's in-flight magazine Enroute.

The name is fittingly tied to the setting. The three owners decided on the enigmatic moniker after witnessing a wolf emerge from the fog while they were out on a fishing trip.

he spacious, window-accentuated contemporary decor of the two-storey setting evokes an air of casual modernity that would not be out of place in downtown Vancouver, yet is very much

Tofino. Be it the hanging star-burst surfboard cluster, hulking waves on the big screen, or the view from patio and window, it exudes an airy, West Coast feel.

The local flavours in its menu are in keeping with the creative liquor in-fusions produced by bar manager Hailey Pasemko, who draws from the environs to present offerings such as Salal Berry Gin, Cedar Strip Rye, a nectarine liquor, Smoked Salmon vodka and a fig-infused rye going by the tag Hailey's Cream. Each complements the taps, which bring to the palate the brews of Driftwood, Hoyne and Phillips craft breweries out of Victoria, plus Tofino's own craft contribution.

The small, street-level Den offers patio, table-and-chair and bar seating in a "let the outside in" atmosphere, while the upper level offers more of the same on a grander scale. High wood ceilings with open beams and wrap-around windows welcome patrons to an airy space enriched by the works of aspiring and successful artists, local and from afar. The Broken Surfboard sculpture by local artist Tammye Shymko, a charcoal wave by New York artist Robert Longo, and Driftwood Wolf carving by Guthrie Gloag join the carved-wood tap handles in an integration of art, theme, and place.

Some 150 seats, including table and bar seating, are complemented by a 14-foot communal table. The Wolf in the Fog proves you can incor-porate upscale contemporary decor and service with the casualness that exemplifies Tofino and the nature-embracing West Coast culture.

Earning your beer
Not far away, but demanding at least the use of a bicycle, sprawl the MacKenzie, Chesterman and Cox Beaches, where you can walk or bike for ages watching surfers, clad in black wetsuits like frolicking Ninjas, and the invariable host of beach visitors dotting horizon and shore. Waves, even on a calm day, explode against rocky shores or distant reefs. You can close your eyes here and confidently take a picture in any direction, knowing you will get a good shot. Explore the galleries of Tofino and its funky shops, with the seemingly endless surfboard images. There are whale-watching tours, tours to "Cougar Annie's" homestead, oceanside hot springs tours, and more. Check out tour-ismtofino.com for a host of activities. Tofino, a world-class destination, has an event or festival in 11 months of the year. Not surprisingly, this includes surfing championships.

ESTABLISHMENT 82

Tofino Brewing Company

691 Industrial Way, Tofino

	1-250-725-2899
Webpage –	tofinobrewingco.com
Services –	wheelchair-accessible with wheelchair-accessible washrooms

Location
On Industrial Way, just south of the town of Tofino

What makes Tofino Brewing Company unique: their beer, dog-friendly, community commitment

From the outside it looked like a large garage; but inside it was like Forest Gump's box of chocolates. You don't know what you are getting until you open the box.

That this is a serious brewing company operation there can be no doubt but resting amidst it all is a comfortably inviting bar where children and families are welcomed and a host of self-brewed beverages are available. It does not provide food services but patrons can order in, a service provided by the Red Can Gourmet and PicNic Charcuterie.

Beverages are unique in name and composition such as Kelp Stout (made with real kelp), Spruce Tree Ale (conditioned with fresh spruce tips) and Dawn Patrol Coffee Porter (using locally baked coffee beans and soaked vanilla beans) to name but a few. At any one time there are twelve taps on the go and a single one

dedicated to a unique, virtually non-alcoholic drink, Kombucha (a fermented tea)

The bar inserted into this brewing operation is cleanly functional, spacious and inviting with stool seating and ample elbow room. Who would have thought a concrete bar would marry so well with wood, stained and paint. Capacity seats 35.

Throughout the venue the walls are decorated with prints by local artist Alexandra Ewen

Any doubt that Tofino Brewing Company perceives itself as an integral part of the West Coast from Ucluelet to Tofino would be set to rest by its contributions to many local charities.

Since opening in April 2011, Tofino Brewing has managed to establish a reputation throughout Vancouver Island, with its products widely carried.

And like Forest's box of chocolates, there are so many surprises to chose from.

Earning your beer
Within a 10-minute walk or a short drive up Industrial Way, and well signposted, is the trailhead for the Tonquin Beach Trail, which leads you through West Coast rainforest to wide, sandy Tonquin Beach, strewn with sea-washed boulders, sand modelled by the surf, and long, rocky fingers pointing out to sea. There is ample room to explore while being serenaded by the roar of the white-crested surf.

The beach and trail make about an hour-long return trip for refreshments at the brewing company, but chances are you will want to spend a goodly portion of time exploring the beach once you get there.
Other hiking trails lead off from the main trail. Check tonquintrail.ca for more details.

SECTION EIGHT North Island

ESTABLISHMENT 83

Old Saltery Pub

Telegraph Cove

	1-250-928-3155
Webpage –	telegraphcoveresort.com
Services –	wheelchair-accessible with wheelchair-accessible washrooms

Location
Telegraph Cove is 16 kilometres on paved road, off of Highway #19 heading to Port Hardy. Well signposted.

<u>What makes the Old Saltery unique:</u> view, setting, history, architecture, location

A living monument to a bygone era, the Old Saltery Pub recalls a coastal lifestyle gone but not forgotten. It is part of Telegraph Cove Resort, a restored fishing and logging town that's the result of visionary thinking and as evocative as Barkerville.

Telegraph Cove naturally draws its name from its beginnings as a station on a telegraph line, but what brought it some measure of permanence was its evolution into a fishing cannery and village, founded in part with Japanese investments. When the prosperous days of fishing and logging passed, the village, with its boardwalk main street and seasoned buildings, seemed destined to collapse into the arms of the sea. That is, until Gordie and Marilyn Graham bought it in its entirety, over 30 years ago, and created an internationally renowned resort, of which the old village and its history are a major attraction.

The original fish saltery

was rebuilt to specifications and today houses both the Killer Whale Cafe and the Old Saltery Pub. The open and airy pub affords indoor seating at tables, bar, and along the outside deck overlooking the busy little cove, where one is apt to spy a foraging bear, soaring heron and more while enjoying a meal and refreshments. Historical artifacts include an old rowboat (courtesy of Rivers Inlet) resting below the open-framed ceiling with its exposed tin roof, as well as a retired three-ton engine and a working organ. There are shelves lined with artifacts, wall-sized historical photos from the saltery's past, a large copper-topped fireplace surrounded by a bar-height table and chairs, Van Isle sail race banners suspended from the upper walls, and sea views flooding through the many windows. Patrons coming in through the stained-glass front doors enter a woody interior filled with light, and the hall connecting the restaurant and pub is lined with photos of the people and history of the village.

A walk along the main street boardwalk takes you past colourfully restored buildings, each carrying a plaque with its own story, put to work as accommodations. There's a Whale Interpretive Centre, offices and staff housing before you reach a breathtaking view out over Johnstone Strait. Here you will read about a French tourist ripping an old oar from a tree that had grown around it, to save Buddy the dog from the clutches of a cougar, and other people who brought life to this special place. The renovated village is wheelchair-friendly and offers wi-fi to those renting cabins and houses. The pub hours tend to be influenced by the number of patrons wishing to remain past regular hours. The resort services also include a coffee shop, general store and a 125-spot serviced RV and camping site within a kilometre.

Favoured Island products on tap include Longwood's from Nanaimo and Merridale Cider from Cobble Hill. Joining them is famed Guinness. Spending at least one evening here in one of the rooms or cabins gives you the opportunity to relate to the stories of the people who lived and worked here. There's plenty of atmosphere to appreciate as you savour the pub offerings while gazing over the busy little cove below. Here is living proof that heritage, environmental responsibility, and beauty can co-exist in a commercial endeavour.

It is no wonder Telegraph Cove is internationally acclaimed and visited.

Earning your beer

There is a raft of things to do at the cove. From exceptional whale-watching tours (featuring more than whales), grizzly bear tours over to Knight Inlet on the mainland, the Whale Interpretive Centre, eco-tours, kayaking tours and rentals, to fishing charters, there are ample experiences to warrant a full vacation in this one spot.

If you are up to burning a few calories hiking, there is a trail blazed by Gordie Graham and his friend, the late Dave Farrant, which takes you 2.5 kilometres (roughly a three-hour round trip) to Blinkhorn Point, with viewpoints and beach access along the way. Once named the Blinkhorn Trail, it has been renamed in Dave Farrant's honour.
Make sure to check out the website telegraphcoveresort.com and its links to tours and services.

And, if you get a chance to chat with Gordie while he is barbecuing salmon for patrons, there are many more stories and suggestions to be had.

ESTABLISHMENT 84

The Whale's Rub Pub

The Oceanfront Hotel, 210 1st Street, Sointula, Malcolm Island
1-250-230-6722
Webpage – theoceanfronthotel.ca
Services – wi-fi, wheelchair-accessible with wheelchair-accessible washroom

Location
Visible to your immediate left is the dock for the ferry from Port McNeil.

What makes the Whale's Rub Pub unique: view, location, setting, Sointula

Like Sointula, the stubborn little community on Malcolm Island a 25-minute ferry ride from Port McNeil, the Oceanfront Hotel and the Whale's Rub Pub are survivors.

The present ownership of the pub and hotel dates to 1977, following a series of operators since the complex's inception in 1974. In 2000, the former Bilge Pub, famed for its coziness, was moved upstairs to larger quarters, accommodating 155 patrons. A naming contest in 2006 brought it the moniker it carries to this day—fitting because, out at Bere Point, there is a beach where orcas take delight in gliding along the pebbly shore, rubbing themselves. They are not loath to let visitors watch their whale rub from shore, should you be so lucky as to catch them in the act.

The Rub is a rustic, eclectic setting oriented visually to the sea (Broughton Strait), which is an ever-present sight, whether viewed through large windows or from the sheltered or open deck areas. Inside, a ded-

(photo courtesy Oceanfront Hotel)

icated stage and dance floor are surrounded by ample seating, at the bar and at tables. A pool table niche with a large five-by-nine-foot table provides for a greater challenge. The atmosphere is enriched with 30 years of collected antiques and local findings, a functioning jukebox, a piano available for those tempted to tickle the ivories, and an informal honour-system library that houses several thousand books, where a patron can ease back in a leather chair and take a read.

Victoria's craft brewery Phillips has an honoured place on the taps, and live entertainment is part of the package. Thursdays are turned over to open-mic nights, and numerous local events spill over into the pub. Halloween events, ball tournaments, the Salmon Days Festival and Winter Fest are all excuses for celebration.

As well there is Finnvasion, a unique group from Finland that has visited Sointula with some frequency and put on performances in the local community hall. These entertainers have shared their talents with the Rub's patrons.

Adjacent to the pub are a pet-friendly hotel (where you can go to sleep and wake up to the rhythm of the ocean outside your window) and a cold beer and wine store.

Economic hard times in logging and fishing have affected Sointula, now just a vestige of what was once envisaged as a Finnish Utopian community, but it is more than a shadow of its past. It and the Rub remain vibrant and very much a community worth a special visit.

Earning your beer

There is so much to do and see here, and a free bike-loan system available to do it with. You can pick up a bike at the Sointula Resource Centre, across from the ferry, and set about cruising the island's quite level roads to experience the town and the beauty of the coastline.

Hikers can take the 1.5-mile Mateoja Heritage Trail right from town, or bike to the start of the six-mile Beautiful Bay Trail on the other side of the narrow isle, where you can see the giant sitka (212 feet) and Puoli Vali canyon. Explorers can visit the old cemetery and look for markers of the Finnish pioneers before biking or driving the scenic Kaleva Road route to enjoy vistas of Vancouver Island, Cormorant Island and, by chance, some common sea life.

The surrounding waters and beaches are famed for their fishing, clamming, crabbing, scuba diving, kayaking and boating. Bird watching is popular enough for there to be a local club. (mibirdclub.wordpress.com)

It is well worthwhile to visit the local museum to learn about Sointula's romantic past, when star-struck idealists from Finland put their heart into establishing a Utopian community on these idyllic shores (where the micro-climate is said to be more akin to the southern Gulf Islands than Northern Vancouver Island). Its brief existence began in 1901, however many of the settlers stayed after the community formally disbanded, and they left a lasting impact upon the island.

"Place of Harmony" Sointula has persisted beyond its founders. It is so safe a place it lost its police force, and its pub prides itself on being a safe and relaxing oasis. Visit the Rub. Visit Sointula.
Worth the trip.

Check vancouverislandnorth.ca/communities/sointula.

ESTABLISHMENT 85

The Quarterdeck Pub

655 Hardy Bay Road, Port Hardy
1-250-949-6922
Webpage – quarterdeckresort.net
Services – wi-fi, wheelchair-accessible with wheelchair-accessible washrooms

<u>Location</u>
Hugging the waterfront along Hardy Bay Road heading south from town, the Quarterdeck Pub sits in solitude across the drive from the Quarterdeck Inn.

<u>What makes the Quarterdeck unique:</u> setting, location, view

The contemporary feel of the Quarterdeck Pub proves you don't need age to establish a "fisherman's pub" atmosphere. Here, within sight and sound of fishing fleets both commercial and chartered, the pub comfortably accommodates patrons running the gamut from maritimers to international visitors, both drawn by the allure of the sea.

The spacious interior has two separate rooms, one graced with a gas fireplace and the other kitty-corner to the bar, an entertainment area with a pool table and darts, and a bright, glass-enclosed sunroom offering a full view of the bay and fishing fleet. An interior false roof harbours a dry-land rowboat for effect, and the walls are hung with photos of some of the local fishing boats.

Now more than 20 years old, the pub has changed hands several times. It's now part of a hotel/marina/pub complex that offers access to charter fishing options. A big part of the international draw is the nearby ferry to Prince Rupert, which takes wayfarers up the dramatic Inside Passage.

The resort marina offers 1,000 feet of moorage and can accommodate craft up to 150 feet. The seaplane base is close by. Wheelchair-accessible, the Quarterdeck also affords live entertainment on occasion. And, it is child-friendly until 9 p.m.

The six taps serve products of Victoria's Vancouver Island Breweries, including Piper's Pale Ale and 19 IPA. Here, close to the waterside and a working boat marina, the life of the sea is little more than a breath away.

Earning your beer
Within walking distance is the head of the Harbourfront Walking Trail, which can take you to the Hardy Bay Estuary and/or up the Quatse Trail Loop, where you can visit the Quatse Salmon Stewardship Centre. The hikes offer viewing of abundant wildlife, birds and marsh vegetation. Pick up a city map showing the trails from the front desk of the Quarterdeck Inn or the the tourist information centre (7250 Market Street; 866-427-3901).

The centre also has information on activities such as viewing murals and totems, the local museum, numerous hikes in the region and the FILOMI festival (annual event celebrating the foundation industries of fishing, logging and mining, which runs the second weekend of July). The resort webpage offers links to whale-watching operations, grizzly bear tours, sport fishing charters, kayaking, eco-tours and scuba diving. The water taxi service opens up many of these features and provides access to the famed Cape Scott and North Coast trails for those entertaining serious hiking ventures.

EPILOGUE

In researching a book like Amber River I got to see a different side of an evolving attitude towards social drinking.

Recalling an era when taverns required women to attend with escorts and serious drinking was the norm for both drinkers and servers the attitude shift is dramatic. Certainly there remain taverns and bars where some old patterns persist but with the neighbourhood pub and changing times there is a marked evolution.

The arrival of the craft beer culture has seen a new breed of beer aficionados acquiring knowledge and expectations not dissimilar to wine lovers.

Brew pubs are thriving, particularly in Victoria, but also up Island.

Food services are not unusually topping alcohol as the prime product in many a pub.

Community involvement and participation is often apparent in fund raising events

To this is added a more responsible attitude towards alcohol consumption as attested to by a number of establishments offering rides home by bus or car or having arrangements with taxis.

And, as for exploring things to do in the immediate vicinity and nearby environs of the respective pubs I can only say I but scraped the tip of the ice berg. There seems an almost endless supply of such in and around Vancouver Island and the teeming Salish Sea.